CLASSIC
for CLOCKS
WOODWORKERS

CLASSIC
for CLOCKS
WOODWORKERS

COMPLETE PATTERNS FOR 21 CLOCKS

RAYMOND HAIGH

CASSELL

*All the line illustrations have been
drawn by the author*

Cassell
Wellington House
125 Strand
London WC2R OBB

First published 1994
First paperback edition 1996

Distributed in the United States
by Sterling Publishing Co., Inc.
387 Park Avenue South, New York, NY 10016-8810

Distributed in Australia
by Capricorn Link (Australia) Pty Ltd
2/13 Carrington Road, Castle Hill, NSW 2154

British Library Cataloguing-in-Publication Data
A catalogue record for this book is available from the British Library

ISBN 0-304-34831-7

Typeset by Litho Link Ltd, Welshpool, Powys, UK

Printed and bound in Slovenia by Mariborski tisk
by arrangement with Korotan Ljubljana

Contents

Introduction

I hope that both amateur and professional craftsmen will find clock cases to their liking in this book. Chronologically, the collection spans five centuries – from the Renaissance to the Art Deco period – and geographically it encompasses both the Old World and the New.

I have not slavishly copied museum pieces. Dials, hands and brassware currently retailed do not permit this, and the large size of some antique clocks can make them seem out of place in modern homes. Instead, I have taken care to identify the proportions and typical details of the various styles of case and to select the most appropriate dials and fittings from the range available. This, together with hand-crafting techniques, imparts an authenticity which is frequently lacking in factory-made reproductions, and the clocks harmonize well with period settings.

Although some of the cases have been scaled down in size, typical dimensions of the original antiques are included, and guidance is given, so that larger versions can be produced should this be desired.

I have also included cases which were more usually constructed of metal. Perfection of shape and form rather than materials gives these designs their particular appeal, and for this reason I have interpreted them here in wood.

Set upon a mantelpiece or a table, many of the clocks become eye-catching conversation pieces, and brief notes on the history and derivation of all of the designs have been given so that informed comment can be made.

The clocks incorporate quartz-regulated movements. These devices are small, robust, accurate, reliable and inexpensive. Their use has made possible the scaling down of the larger cases and the faithful reproduction of American clocks which have a pendulum located just behind the front panel.

I have also described the construction of a simple moon dial mechanism. Powered by a quartz movement, it is compact enough to be incorporated into the break-arch dials of some of the bracket clocks featured in the collection here.

Special tools and equipment do not have to be purchased. Full details are included of simple and inexpensive home-constructed tools which overcome the problem of obtaining mouldings and turnings, and greatly ease the production of accurate mitres and curved shapes. A method of simulating boxwood and ebony inlays, or stringing, which produces results that are virtually indistinguishable from the real thing, is also given.

I hope these simple tools and labour-saving techniques will be of interest even to experienced craftsmen with fully equipped workshops. Along with some basic guidance, they have been included to encourage anyone with ability in the use of tools to construct clocks which rival the quality of mass-produced items, often sold for more than ten times the cost of materials and parts.

ACKNOWLEDGEMENTS

I am indebted to Mr S. Mitchell, Curator of the American Clock and Watch Museum, Bristol, Connecticut; David Thompson, Superintendent of the Horological Students' Room, the British Museum, London; Gareth Williams, Curator of Furniture and Woodwork at the Victoria and Albert Museum, London; Michelle Petyt, Assistant at the Geffrye Museum, London; Peter Cormack, Deputy Keeper, the William Morris Gallery, Walthamstow, London; and Stella Beddoe, Keeper of Decorative Art, the Royal Pavilion Art Gallery and Museums, Brighton, all of whom took the time to supply me with the dimensions of clocks and dials in their care. I am also indebted to Mr M. Newcombe of Newcombe and Son, Clockmakers, London, for his observations on the development of the Admiral's Hat or Napoleon clock.

PART ONE

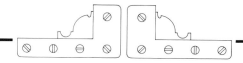

CHAPTER ONE

Materials, Tools and Equipment

MATERIALS USED IN THE CONSTRUCTION OF THE CASES

The following paragraphs refer only to the timbers, veneers and adhesives used in the construction of the case shells. Dials, handles, decorative brassware and finishing materials are dealt with in later chapters.

Timber: Moisture Content

Proper seasoning is important. Cases displayed on a mantelpiece above a heating appliance are subjected to intense drying out, and shrinkage and cracking will result if the timber used does not have a low moisture content. If in any doubt, store the blocks, turning blanks and rough-cut case parts in the room where the clock is to be located for a few months prior to assembly.

Timber in Strip or Board Form

Softwood should not present any problems, but difficulty may be encountered in obtaining hardwood of the required $\frac{3}{8}$ in or $\frac{1}{2}$ in (9 mm or 13 mm) thickness, in 3 in or 4 in (75 mm or 100 mm) wide strips or wider boards, off the shelf. Stockists can sometimes be persuaded to run blocks or planks which have been purchased from them through their

circular saw, and hand-cutting is not out of the question with the short lengths required. Alternatively, the cases can be constructed of plywood and veneered.

Timber in Block Form

No difficulty should be experienced in obtaining softwoods and common hardwoods in block form. Specialist firms which supply to wood-turners are a reliable source if local timber merchants are unhelpful.

Plywood

Select good-quality material with well-bonded layers. Try and match the colour of the plywood to the colour of the case veneer so that, after staining, any unveneered areas (e.g. the base and back of the case) are not too obtrusive.

Again, $\frac{3}{8}$ in or $\frac{1}{2}$ in (9 mm or 13 mm) thick material should be used, even for the smaller clocks. This makes jointing easier and imparts a feeling of solidity to the cases.

Veneer

Most of the woods used in clock-case making are readily available as veneer. The more exotic woods can be expensive when purchased in full leaves, which are between 7 and 11 ft (2 and 3 metres) long, but many

supply houses sell short leaves and packs of offcuts, which can yield more than enough material for single clocks.

Timber and Veneer Suppliers

Most constructors will be able to make local purchases of pine and plywood. If hardwoods and veneer are not stocked locally, the numerous mail-order suppliers who advertise in craft and woodworking magazines will be able to assist.

Choice of Species

Personal taste and a desire to match other furnishings are, quite properly, likely to be deciding factors, and the method of finishing can have as great an effect on final appearance as the species chosen.

When exotic veneers are being considered, give some thought to the need to obtain identical, or close-matching, timber for the mouldings and turned parts. This can inhibit choice.

Guidance is given later on what is traditionally appropriate for each of the clock designs. The timbers used here were pine, Brazilian and Honduras mahogany, satinwood, cedar of Lebanon, pearwood, ramin and oak. (Ramin was used only for the bun feet on pine clocks and the scotia mouldings on a painted case.) The veneers were mahogany, harewood (sycamore dyed grey with ferrous sulphate), red and black chemically dyed material and makore.

American Timbers

North American timbers are similar to those grown in Europe. American white oak is preferable to the red, and American hard maple should be used rather than the soft variety, which is prone to a pencil-streak-like marking. American craftsmen who prefer walnut have their own native black variety and, if they have no aversion to softwoods for clock-case making, they could try using their southern yellow pine.

Basswood (also known as American lime) and North American tulipwood, both of which work, finish and stain well, would make excellent substitutes for ramin. Closer proximity could also make Honduras mahogany more readily available to American case makers; it is very much the preferred wood of that particular species.

Australian Timbers

The range of timbers grown in Australia is very extensive and the State Reafforestation Policy includes the planting of some European species.

Tasmanian oak (strictly speaking, a type of eucalyptus) would substitute for European or American oak. Tasmanian blackwood is rather like rosewood, and Queensland walnut (again, strictly speaking, not a true walnut) would be the natural choice if a wood of this kind is preferred. Australian craftsmen could try substituting myrtle for mahogany, but this species is not noted for its stability and careful seasoning would be required.

The scratch stock with a selection of blades and mouldings. The larger mouldings are built up from separate pieces

Adhesives

White PVA adhesive, which consists of an emulsion of polyvinyl acetate in water, is used to glue the cases, frames and mouldings. The initial set takes place in about thirty minutes at room temperature and the adhesive develops a strong bond after a few hours. It does not have any gap-filling ability, and joint strength depends on a close fit between the parts. (Examples are Evo-Stik Resin 'W' and Uni Bond Super Strong Woodworker Adhesive.)

Small pieces of veneer are best laid with a petroleum-based impact adhesive. These adhesives contain toluene, and the manufacturer's warnings regarding ventilation and flammability must be strictly observed. Wood dyes and french polishes used in finishing can act as a solvent for this adhesive, but no problems were encountered, even on exposed glue lines. (Examples are Evo-Stik Impact Adhesive and Dunlop Thixofix.)

Metal Fixings

Resist the temptation to use nails or pins to secure mouldings or exposed case parts. The subsequent punching down and hole-stopping will spoil the appearance of the clocks.

ESSENTIAL TOOLS

Many of the items listed here are extremely commonplace, but they have been included for the sake of completeness.

1 steel rule and straight edge, 12 in (300 mm)
2 steel tape measure, 36 in (1 metre)
3 try square, 9 in (230 mm)
4 marking gauge (see also 31)
5 callipers
6 compasses
7 Stanley knife
8 panel-type handsaw (ten points per inch, 25 mm)
9 coping saw
10 junior hacksaw
11 mitre block
12 smoothing or jack plane with 2 in (50 mm) cutter (Stanley No. 4 or 5; Record No. 04 or 05)
13 firmer chisels, $\frac{1}{4}$ in and $\frac{3}{4}$ in (6 mm and 19 mm)
14 skew chisel, $\frac{1}{2}$ in (13 mm)
15 roughing gouge, $\frac{3}{4}$ in (19 mm)
16 small joiner's mallet
17 fine and medium grit combination oil stone
18 electric drill
19 horizontal-stand attachment for the lathe, disc and drum sander
20 drum-sanding attachment
21 set of twist drills, including a selection of sizes up to $\frac{1}{8}$ in (3 mm)
22 vice
23 four G cramps, 4 in (100 mm) or larger
24 six G cramps, 2 in (50 mm)
25 small and medium screwdrivers
26 wire snips
27 long-nosed pliers
28 small cross-pein hammer, about 4 oz (110 g)
29 awl (a pointed bradawl)
30 a selection of small files: round, flat, and square

DESIRABLE TOOLS

31 cutting gauge (see also 4)
32 straight-handled tenon saw (fourteen or more points per inch, 25 mm)
33 bow saw or keyhole saw
34 circular saw attachment for the electric drill
35 block plane, preferably with an adjustable mouth (Stanley No. $9\frac{1}{2}$ G or Record No. $09\frac{1}{2}$)
36 firmer chisel, 1 in (25 mm)
37 model-maker's electric drill or Archimedean drill
38 adjustable bevel, 9 in (230 mm)

Notes on the Above Items

The marking gauge (4) is used mainly for cutting shallow glazing rebates. A cutting gauge (31) is preferable if one can be obtained.

The compasses (6) are required for setting out curved cases. The draughtsman's compasses listed in Chapter Four can be substituted for joiner's compasses.

The bow saw (33) is required only for cutting out the curved profiles of solid-block cases, and an alternative cutting technique is described later. If a bow saw is not available, a keyhole saw will form the movement chambers in solid cases more quickly than the coping saw (9). A circular saw attachment (34) for the electric drill will take much of the effort out of cutting strips for mouldings. It can be substituted for the handsaw (8).

The final planing of the assembled cases will be easier with a block plane (35), which is held in one hand. The models listed have an adjustable mouth (blade opening). Closed down, it reduces the tendency of the wood to rupture when the plane is being used on end grain.

Similarly, either of the small drills (37) will be found more convenient

when making fine holes, and the adjustable bevel (38) will aid the setting out and checking of the sharp Gothic case parts (Chapter Fifteen).

DISC SANDER, DRUM SANDER AND LATHE

A rigid disc sander greatly simplifies the task of forming perfect mitres and, if the balloon and Napoleon clocks are to be constructed (Chapters Eleven and Eighteen), a rigidly mounted drum sander will enable the concave curves to be finished quickly and accurately. A simple lathe is also needed to produce the bun feet and decorative turnings which are fitted to some of the clocks.

Tools of this kind are not so common in amateur workshops, and a simple, home-constructed machine which combines all three functions is described in the Appendix. The prototype was made in half a day, largely from scrap materials, and was used to form the mitres, sand the curves and produce the turnings for all of the cases included in this collection. Constructors with modest workshop facilities ought not, therefore, to be discouraged from attempting any of the clocks.

THE SCRATCH STOCK

For centuries, cabinet-makers have been using this simple tool to run beads and small mouldings. Superseded by moulding planes and, in more recent times, by mechanical cutters, it is now found mainly in the toolboxes of furniture restorers.

The scratch stock removes wood by a scraping rather than a cutting action, and it cannot be used across the grain. Although there are examples of this tool having produced or finished fairly large mouldings, it

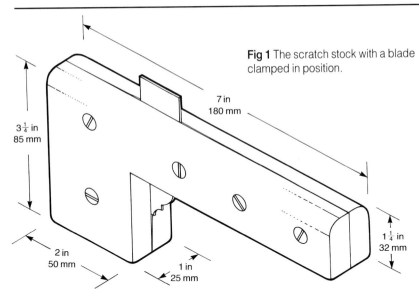

Fig 1 The scratch stock with a blade clamped in position.

becomes increasingly difficult to use when sections exceed 1 × 1 in (25 × 25 mm). These limitations are not a drawback as far as making clock cases is concerned.

Materials for the Scratch Stock
- Two off $\frac{1}{2}$ in (13 mm) thick plywood or hardwood, $7\frac{1}{4} \times 3\frac{1}{2}$ in (185 × 90 mm): these dimensions, which are not critical, include an allowance of $\frac{1}{4}$ in (6 mm) for waste in cutting and finishing
- Five off 1 in (25 mm) No. 12 countersunk steel screws
- Sections of old saw blade for scrapers

Constructing the Scratch Stock
Fig. 1 shows the assembled scratch stock with a scraper tightly sandwiched between the two L-shaped members. Construction should proceed as follows.

① Cut out the two L-shaped pieces, keeping the inner edges true and square. Clamp them together, mark out the screw positions and drill $\frac{1}{8}$ in (3 mm) thread holes through both. If hardwood is used, the thread-hole diameter may need increasing slightly to avoid splitting.

② Part the pieces and enlarge the holes in one of them to $\frac{1}{4}$ in (6 mm). Countersink the enlarged holes and screw the two halves of the tool together.

③ Remove any roughness and protruding screw points, and round all of the external corners. Some effort has to be applied when using the tool, and this rounding and smoothing will make it easier on the hands.

Cutting the Scratch Stock Blades
Blades for small beads and mouldings can be formed from lengths of hacksaw blade. Blades for larger mouldings will require sections cut from old handsaws or similar thin sheet steel. A high degree of tempering makes cutting and shaping material of this kind difficult, but it can be done if a fresh hacksaw blade and sharp files are used. A much easier method is illustrated in Fig. 2 and described below.

① Mount the electric drill in the lathe (see Appendix), fit an abrasive, metal-cutting disc and arrange the tool rest so that it just clears it.

② Holding the sheet steel on the tool

rest, feed it on to the disc and cut out a blade-sized piece.

③ Mark out the scraper profile, remembering that it is the reverse of the moulding section. Allow for clamping the sides as well as the tops of deeper blades into the handle.

④ Apply the piece of steel to the abrasive disc. Remove waste material by means of a series of parallel cuts and then nibble as close as possible to the required profile (see Fig. 2). The small pieces of steel quickly heat up and they should be gripped with pliers for prolonged cutting. Any slight loss of hardness resulting from the heating is not important in this application.

⑤ File the blades to the final profile. Every mark on the blade will be reproduced in the wood, so they should be reasonably well finished.

The above process takes longer to describe than it does to execute. With this method, quite complicated blades can be produced in a few minutes with a little practice. Guidance on the use of the scratch stock is given in Chapter Two.

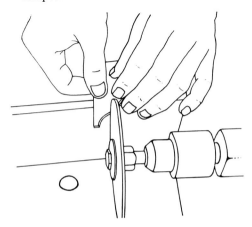

Fig 2 Forming scratch stock blades on a metal cutting disc.

CHAPTER TWO

Using the Tools and Getting a Good Finish

SAFETY MEASURES

Appropriate safety measures must be observed when using power tools. Avoid loose clothing, which could get caught up in moving parts, and wear safety goggles at all times and a face mask when power-sanding operations are creating dust.

USING THE LATHE

The guidance given here has been prepared with the home-made combination machine described in the Appendix very much in mind.

Turning Methods
Cutting and scraping are the two ways of removing wood on a lathe. Cutting requires considerable skill but scraping is far less demanding. All of the turnings depicted in this book were produced by scraping.

Some authorities maintain that the scraping technique cannot be adopted for soft woods, especially those with an uneven grain density. It is certainly difficult to obtain satisfactory results on small-diameter pine items. This is why ramin is recommended for the bun feet on pine cases. The pine dome on the Renaissance clock (Chapter Seven) was, however, turned by scraping.

Success depends on turning the items to within about $\frac{1}{16}$ in (1.5 mm) of the final size and then finishing down to the desired profile with abrasive paper.

Preparing the Wood for the Lathe
Mark the centres at both ends as accurately as possible. The lathe described in the Appendix will accept square-section material up to about $1\frac{1}{4} \times 1\frac{1}{4}$ in (32 × 32 mm). Above this size it is desirable to remove corners, planing the wood to an octagonal section, and long cylinders should be limited to about 2 in (50 mm) finished diameter. Short lengths of material above about 3 in (75 mm) diameter (e.g. circular clock cases and domes) should be brought to a near cylindrical form on the disc sander before being turned to their final shape on the lathe. This preliminary work will considerably ease the demands on the drill motor. A 5 in (125 mm) diameter circular case is about the largest item the simple drill-powered lathe can reasonably cope with. Two-speed drills should be set to the lowest speed, especially when turning large diameter items.

Mounting Wood in the Lathe
Turnings are held in the headstock (the drill chuck) by means of a steel wood screw with its head removed. Vary the gauge of the screw to suit the size of the item. The dome for the Renaissance clock requires a 2 in (50 mm) No. 10 or No. 12 screw. The slender pillars of the American pillar and scroll clock or the turnings on the

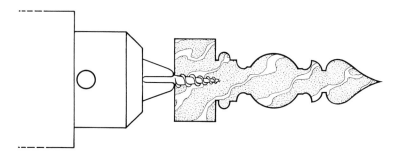

Fig 3 Finials for the sharp Gothic clock are held only in the drill chuck to permit turning to a point.

sharp Gothic clock (Chapter Fifteen) require $1\frac{1}{4}$ in (32 mm) No. 8 screws.

Form thread holes for the screws. When preparing small-diameter items, make sure these holes are large enough to prevent splitting, and that the piece of wood is long enough to enable all scraping to be kept away from the screw. Fig. 3 makes this clear.

The pointed and threaded rod in the tailstock acts as the other pivot. Use the awl to form a sinking for the point and screw the rod into it reasonably firmly. Lock the rod with the locking screw. The rod may need tightening from time to time, as the work proceeds.

Small finials, such as those on the sharp Gothic clock, are held in the chuck of the drill only. This permits turning to a point (see Fig. 3).

Locating the Tool Rest

Always keep the tool rest as close as possible to the surface of the wood being turned. Failure to do this can result in the scraper or chisel handle being flung upwards by the rotating wood. Fig. 4 shows the rest arranged for turning the crown of a dome or the beaded front rim of a drum. Note the notch cut into the top of the rest to clear the tailstock centre: the rest vertical member should be renewed after carrying out turning operations of this kind.

Using the Roughing Gouge to Turn a Cylinder

Square stock is reduced to a cylindrical shape by means of the roughing gouge. With the back of the tool pressed on to the headstock end of the tool rest, bring the gouge into contact with the rotating wood and move it towards the tailstock, pointing it slightly in the direction of travel. Run the gouge backwards and

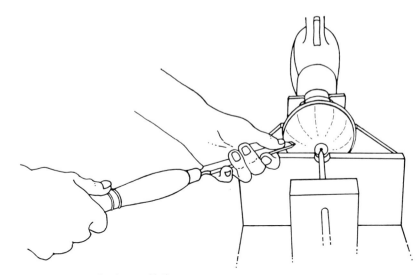

Fig 4 Scraping the crown of a dome with the tool rest fixed across the bed of the home-made lathe.

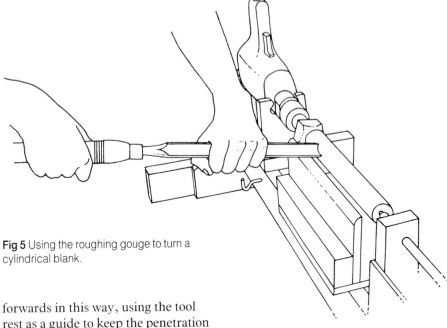

Fig 5 Using the roughing gouge to turn a cylindrical blank.

forwards in this way, using the tool rest as a guide to keep the penetration of the gouge constant, until a cylinder has been turned (see Fig. 5). Finish off with abrasive paper.

Marking Out the Turning

Lay a strip of paper on the full-size detail and mark on it the boundaries of beads, flats and grooves. Lay the strip on the cylinder in the lathe and transfer the marks (see Fig. 6). Extend the marks by rotating the cylinder while a pencil is held in contact with it. With the lathe running, apply the skew chisel to the marks to form a cut line (see Fig. 7). This will survive the turning operation until the basic shape has begun to be established.

Use callipers to check and, if necessary, match the diameters of the various parts of the turnings.

Scrapers

Scrapers can be made from old files, chisels, screwdrivers or any hard steel stock in suitable sizes. To make a scraper, simply grind the end to a shallow angle: 70° to 80° is about right. Use a coarse sanding disc in the drill if a grinder is not available. The burr produced by grinding enhances the scraping action. Fig. 8 makes this clear.

Scrapers can become quite hot in use, so withdraw the tip from the work frequently to prevent overheating, and regrind them from time to time.

The turnings illustrated throughout the book were produced using an old $\frac{1}{8}$ in (3 mm) mortise chisel, a small electrician's screwdriver, a pointed awl and the skew chisel as scrapers. Using a skew chisel in this way would be anathema to a skilled woodturner, but it does work quite well in practice. The chisel should be kept razor-sharp, even when it is being used as a scraper. The point of the awl is used to define bead boundaries, sometimes after the final sanding.

Hold the scraping tool horizontally or inclined slightly downwards, as shown in Fig. 8. Never incline the tool upwards; if you do, it will dig in and ruin the work.

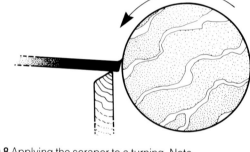

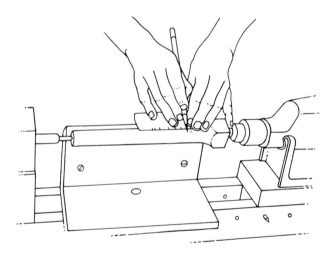

Fig 6 Using a strip of paper to transfer points on a drawing to a turning blank in the lathe.

Fig 8 Applying the scraper to a turning. Note the downward inclination of the tool and the proximity of the rest to the rotating wood.

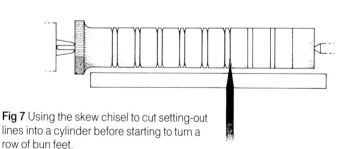

Fig 7 Using the skew chisel to cut setting-out lines into a cylinder before starting to turn a row of bun feet.

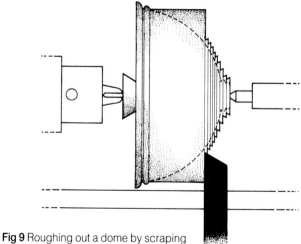

Fig 9 Roughing out a dome by scraping away a series of thin slices.

Turning Complex Shapes

Establish datum depths (e.g. the base, neck and rim of an urn) when turning complex shapes, then link these points with the necessary curve or curves. Remove material by scraping away a series of thin ($\frac{1}{32}$ in or 1 mm) slices, as depicted in Fig. 9.

Abrasives

Use abrasives to smooth the rough surface left by scraping. Work from coarse to fine, holding strips of paper against the rotating wood. Fold the abrasive into narrow strips to clean up grooves and small features.

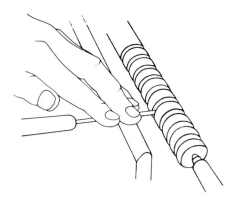

Fig 10 Using a narrow scraper to turn the necks on a row of bun feet.

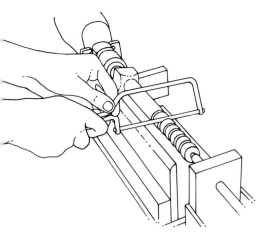

Fig 11 Using a small hacksaw to part finished turnings from the blank.

Turning Bun Feet

Bun feet are best turned in a continuous row along a cylinder of wood, as illustrated in Fig. 10. Turn eight feet and select the four which are the best match. The cylindrical blank should be turned to a sanding thickness more than the outer diameter of the feet.

Parting Turnings from the Blank

Conventionally, a parting chisel is applied to cut completed turnings from the cylindrical blank, but a small hacksaw can be used for this purpose, as illustrated in Fig. 11. Simply hold the saw against the rotating wood and let it cut down until the centre is almost reached. When parting bun feet, take each cut down a little at a time. The cuts can be completed after the cylinder has been removed from the lathe.

USING THE DISC SANDER

Semi-rigid, resin-bonded abrasive discs work well in the sander and have a long life. If these cannot be obtained, cut a 7 in (175 mm) diameter disc from a standard sheet of abrasive paper and secure it in the sander with the large washer and fixing nut.

Even with a medium-grade abrasive, material is removed quickly and a light touch is called for. When sanding curved shapes, keep the wood moving constantly to avoid flats. Fig. 12 shows an item being squared up on the disc, Fig. 13 shows a mitre cut being finished and, in Fig. 14, the top of the Napoleon clock (Chapter Eighteen) is being rounded (take care to avoid large items such as this being marked by the retaining nut and washer). When preparing mitre cuts, mouldings have to be applied to the right, as well as to

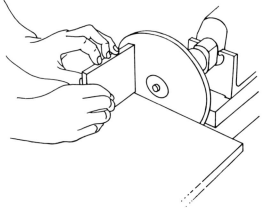

Fig 12 Squaring a piece of wood on the disc sander.

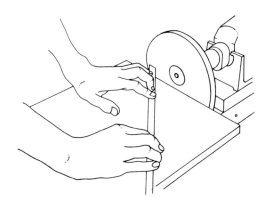

Fig 13 Finishing a mitre cut on the disc sander.

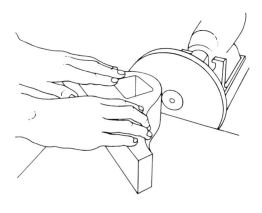

Fig 14 Finishing a convex curve on the disc sander.

the left, of the pivot. If the wood is held firmly, the lifting action of the rotating disc is not a problem.

A fence can be fixed to the sanding table if desired, although this facility was not included here. Instead, a large 45° set square was used to draw a network of guidelines on the table at 45° and 90° to the disc.

USING THE DRUM SANDER

Foam-plastic-filled sanding drums are produced by a number of manufacturers. The tightest curve that can be accommodated is, of course, determined by the diameter of the drum, and 5 in (125 mm) is a widely available size. A drum of this diameter was used to form and finish the concave curves on the clocks in this collection.

The width of the sanding belts is about $2\frac{3}{8}$ in (60 mm). If the depth of the case is greater than this, make a few passes of the drum, then turn the case over and repeat the process. This will almost double the sanding depth and, with a little care and a light touch, there will be no ridge where the passes overlap. Fig. 15 shows the drum sander being used to finish the concave curves on the Napoleon clock.

USING THE SCRATCH STOCK

Fig. 16 shows the scratch stock being used to form a moulding along the edge of a plank of wood. On completion, the moulding is sawn off as a strip and the sawn face planed smooth and true. This is the preferred method for producing mouldings. Heavy pressure can be applied to the scratch stock and the tool can be held in place against the face of the plank.

Fig. 17 shows a moulding being

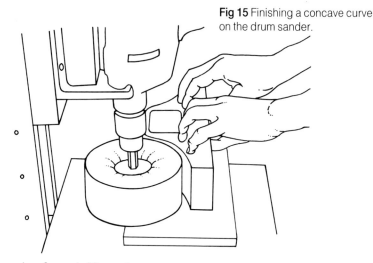

Fig 15 Finishing a concave curve on the drum sander.

run along a strip of wood. Here, the scratch stock is held in a vice, blade uppermost, and the strip of wood pressed on to it as it is moved backwards and forwards to produce the desired profile.

Effort will be saved if as much material as possible is removed with a plane before the scraping operation begins. Initially, the surface of the moulding may seem rough and uneven, especially with soft woods of variable density, such as pine. It is only when the blade has removed the waste material and is beginning to burnish the surface, rather than scrape it, that a perfectly smooth and regular profile emerges.

Always keep the scratch stock blade at right angles to the moulding. If it is skewed, it will gouge into the part-formed beads and ruin the work.

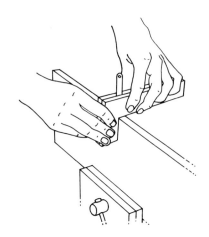

Fig 16 Forming a moulding with the scratch stock.

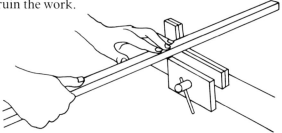

Fig 17 Fix the scratch stock, blade uppermost, in the vice when forming mouldings on thin strips.

VENEERING

Preparing the Groundwork

Groundwork, whether of ply or softwood, must be smooth and free from surface blemishes. All but the smallest defects will ghost through the veneer and stand out after polishing. If moulding pins have been used to hold exposed case parts together (this is recommended only for the American sharp Gothic case), they must be punched down and the holes and any other imperfections filled with plastic-wood-type stopping.

Veneering Simple Box Cases

Cut selected pieces of veneer slightly oversize and spread a film of contact adhesive on one of them and on one of the case sides. Allow the adhesive to become touch-dry (about fifteen to twenty minutes), then lay the veneer on the case, applying firm pressure by hand to ensure a good bond, especially at the edges.

Press the case, veneer face down, on to a cutting board and trim the veneer. Make several light passes rather than one heavy cut, using a sharp Stanley knife or something similar. When cutting across the grain, always work from the outside to the centre of the piece of veneer. If necessary, lightly sand the edges of the veneer flush with the sides of the case, but take care not to round the veneer edges.

Repeat the above process until all exposed faces have been veneered.

Veneering Cases with Curved Sides

With cases of this kind, it is best to lay and trim the veneer to the front first.

If the profile is sharply curved (e.g. the Celtic-influence Art Nouveau clock, Chapter Seventeen), the grain of the veneer on the sides must run from front to back; otherwise it will not bend around the case. Veneer cannot be obtained in long strips with the grain orientated in this way, and a joint has to be formed.

Cut strips of veneer slightly wider than the case depth and mark the location of the joint on the case with a soft pencil. Apply adhesive to the veneer and the case sides and allow it to become touch-dry. Protect the area of the joint with polythene sheet and lay one of the pieces of veneer with its end projecting over the joint line. The polythene will prevent adhesion taking place at the joint for the time being.

Lay the other strip, again with its end projecting over the joint line, then slice through both layers of veneer using a straight edge and a sharp knife. Remove waste veneer and polythene, and press the ends down firmly. If the veneer grain has been selected, cutting through the overlapping ends will result in an imperceptible joint.

Veneer on the Celtic-influence Art Nouveau clock is joined where the top swells out from the sides and at the crown of the case. Begin applying the veneer at the internal angles formed where the top meets the sides, the ends here being pre-cut to fit. Roll and press strips around and over the top, forming the joint at the crown in the manner described above.

Repeat the process down the sides of the case.

Veneering Large Mouldings

The large crown mouldings on the inverted bell top and bell top clocks (Chapter Ten) can be veneered to ensure a good match between top and case, or to obscure a bad match between the various parts of the moulding.

Apply the veneer before the moulding is cut into lengths and mitred. When veneering concave surfaces, wrap and tie the veneer around a dowel of smaller radius than the hollow in the moulding before touching the glued surfaces together. This will help prevent the veneer bridging over. If this happens, the veneer will split when it is pressed down and all of the work expended in producing the moulding will have been wasted.

GETTING A GOOD FINISH

Clocks are often prominently displayed and any flaws are likely to be very noticeable. The following suggestions may help in the quest for a perfect finish.

① Use a Stanley knife to mark out parts prior to sawing. Mark out cross-grain cuts on all faces and on either side of saw lines: this will limit splintering along the saw kerf (see Fig. 18).

② Keep tools razor-sharp and planes lightly set to take fine shavings, especially when finishing cases or working over areas of difficult grain.

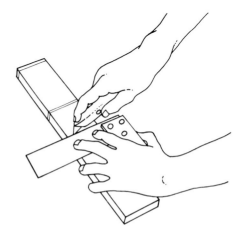

Fig 18 Marking out case parts with a Stanley knife. The cuts on both sides of saw lines limit splintering.

③ Check grain direction before starting work (see Fig. 19). Try planing across the grain in turbulent areas which do not respond to planing along the grain in either direction.

④ When gluing pieces together to form wider strips or larger blocks, always match the grain direction; otherwise it may be impossible to obtain a good finish. Cut all of the pieces from the same length of timber so as to ensure that colour, porosity and moisture content are matched. This is particularly important when building up solid blocks. Colour and porosity need to match to avoid subsequent staining problems, and if moisture content is not constant throughout the block, differential movement will increase the risk of cracking.

⑤ Identical case parts (e.g. the front and back or two sides of a case) should be cut and finished together.

If these parts do not exactly match, right-angle corners and parallel sides cannot be formed. Clamp sheet parts in the vice and plane them true and to size in pairs.

⑥ The profile of a moulding may not be constant throughout its length, even when it has been produced by a machine. To ensure perfect mitres, join pieces together in the sequence in which they are cut from the strip.

⑦ Use softwood slips or thick carpet felt to prevent vice or cramp jaws marking the case parts.

⑧ When small parts have to be trued, apply them to the blade of an inverted plane, as shown in Fig. 20.

⑨ Fig. 21 shows the sole of a plane being used as a vertical guide for sanding small parts. This ensures that edges are flat and square and not rounded by the sanding process.

⑩ When finishing completed cases, avoid blurring the mouldings by indiscriminate sanding. Always use a sanding block when working on flat surfaces and wrap abrasive around a length of dowel when smoothing concave mouldings.

⑪ Frames and boxes can be tested for squareness by checking that the diagonals are equal.

⑫ Obtain the movement, the dial and all of the fittings before commencing the construction of a case. Any minor adjustments to suit these components can then be made before the case parts are marked out.

⑬ Wipe excess PVA adhesive from exposed case areas with a rag dipped in warm, slightly soapy water; otherwise the glue residue will show up as light patches when the case is stained.

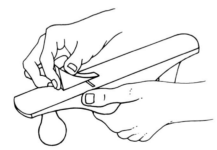

Fig 20 True up and finish small parts on an inverted plane.

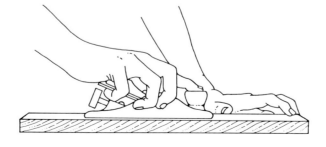

Fig 19 Check the direction of the grain on an adjacent edge before starting to plane a piece of wood.

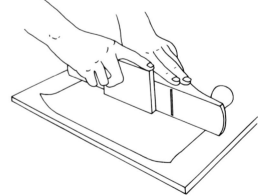

Fig 21 Using a plane as a right-angle guide when sanding the edges of small parts.

CHAPTER THREE

Constructing
the Case Shells

BASIC FORMS OF CONSTRUCTION

The cases are of four basic types: simple boxes; glass-fronted boxes; blocked-out boxes and solid block.

Simple and glass-fronted box cases can be constructed from solid wood in strip or board form, or from plywood and then veneered; blocked-out box cases have to be veneered.

SIMPLE BOXES

Constructing the basic box involves the same techniques whether it is formed from strips of solid wood or plywood. An 'exploded' view of this type of case is given in Fig. 22. Construction should proceed in the following stages.

The Basic Box

① Cut out the pieces of solid wood or plywood with a $\frac{1}{8}$ in (3 mm) planing allowance for each sawn edge. If solid wood is being used, plane the outer and inner faces flat, true and smooth, and bring the panels to an even thickness. Lightly plane any machine-finished faces to remove blemishes.

② Take the front and back panels, clamp them together in the vice, and plane the long edges straight, square

and parallel, reducing the pieces to the required width. Repeat the above process with the two side panels.

③ With a long edge aligned, clamp the four front and side pieces together in the vice. Using the try square and Stanley knife, mark out the precise length, then remove them from the

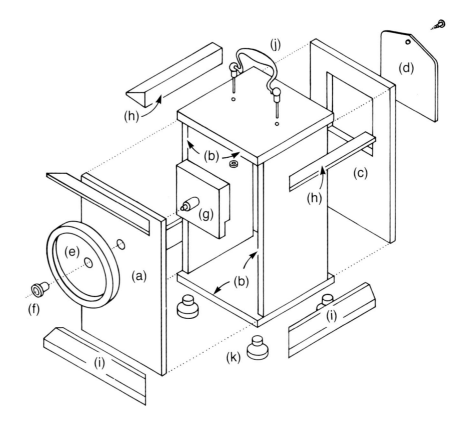

Fig 22 The simple box case: (a) front panel; (b) top, bottom and sides; (c) rear panel; (d) access flap; (e) bezel and dial plate; (f) exposed movement fixing; (g) movement; (h) top mouldings; (i) bottom mouldings; (j) handle; (k) feet.

vice and extend these marks around all four faces of each piece.

④ Plane the ends true and square, leaving them a shaving or two proud of the length marks.

⑤ Mark out and form the spindle hole in the front panel and a sinking for the fixing nut if it is to be hidden behind the dial. Form any necessary sinking for the movement on the inside face of the front panel (to allow the spindle to project sufficiently). Use the coping saw to form the movement access hole in the rear panel.

⑥ Apply PVA adhesive and cramp front, back and sides together. Check that the assembly is square.

⑦ Remove the cramps when the adhesive has hardened and give the case ends a final planing, leaving them true, level and square.

⑧ Apply PVA adhesive and press the slightly oversize top and bottom pieces into position. Use a weight to put the joints under pressure if a large enough cramp is not available.

⑨ Plane away the overhang on the top and bottom pieces, leaving them flush with the sides. Plane away any slight lipping at the joints between the other parts, then smooth the case with fine abrasive paper, leaving it free from blemishes.

⑩ Plywood cases must be veneered at this stage (mouldings are glued down on top of the veneer).

Mouldings and Turned Parts
⑪ Prepare the mouldings and any turnings. (Veneering and producing mouldings and turnings are described in Chapter Two.)

⑫ Using a mitre block, cut the lengths of moulding for the case sides about $\frac{1}{2}$ in (13 mm) longer than the finished size. Present the rough mitre-cuts to the disc sander and sand them smooth, true and to an exact 45° angle.

⑬ Cut the moulding for the case front, again about $\frac{1}{2}$ in (13 mm) oversize. Finish one end on the disc sander, then hold the piece of moulding in place, on the case, and mark the exact length at the other end. Finish this end on the sander, removing smaller and smaller amounts of material as the mark is approached, and checking frequently until the moulding has been sanded down to a perfect fit.

⑭ Gently remove any swarf left by the disc sander, then glue and cramp the mouldings in position.

⑮ Cut away the side mouldings where they project at the rear of the case, then smooth the ends down flush with a finely set plane, working inwards, towards the case, to avoid splitting.

⑯ Glue any feet, domes or other turnings in position.

Final Items
⑰ Make the flap to cover the movement access hole. Mark out, and make thread holes for, the dial-plate fixing screws, the screw for the cover flap and any screws securing decorative brassware or handles.

GLASS-FRONTED BOXES

Glass-fronted box cases are of two types: those with the glazed door overlapping the sides (e.g. basket top, inverted bell top and bell top, Chapters Nine and Ten) and those with the glazed door set between the side panels (e.g. the American and the Arts and Crafts-style clocks, Chapters Fifteen and Sixteen).

Access to winding holes is not, of course, required when battery-powered movements are used, and the glazed doors are glued in position, some being fitted with dummy hinges. If front-winding, spring-driven movements are to be installed, the doors will have to be made operative and fitted with a simple catch.

With the exception of the American pillar and scroll clock and the clock with the moon dial, all of the glass-fronted cases are fitted with rear doors to give access to the movements.

An 'exploded' view of the overlapping-door type of case is given in Fig. 23. Construction should proceed in the following stages.

The Basic Box
① Cut out and plane true, square and to size the sides, top and bottom of the basic box. Identical in width, these parts can be cut from a single strip which has had its edges planed straight, square and parallel.

② Glue and cramp the box parts together, making sure that the assembly is true and square.

Door Frames with Mitred Corners
(Pedimented Architectural and Basket Top Cases)
③ Prepare the door-frame material in one continuous length, making generous allowance for waste. Run

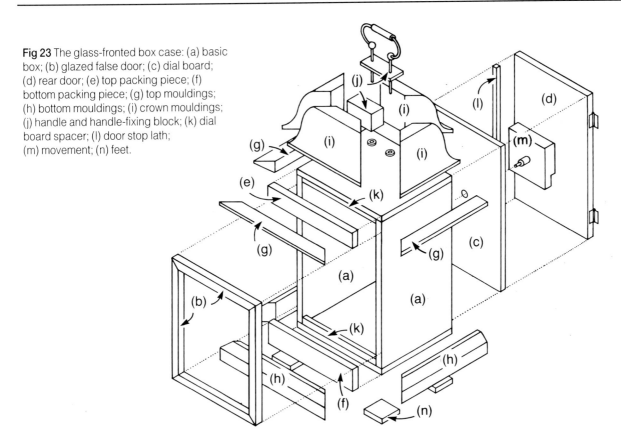

Fig 23 The glass-fronted box case: (a) basic box; (b) glazed false door; (c) dial board; (d) rear door; (e) top packing piece; (f) bottom packing piece; (g) top mouldings; (h) bottom mouldings; (i) crown mouldings; (j) handle and handle-fixing block; (k) dial board spacer; (l) door stop lath; (m) movement; (n) feet.

any beads with the scratch stock, and form the shallow glazing rebate with a marking gauge or cutting gauge. If a marking gauge is used, make the deepest possible grooves, then finish the cuts with a Stanley knife.

④ Using the mitre block, cut the door-frame members about $\frac{1}{2}$ in (13 mm) oversize, then sand the rough cuts smooth, true and to an exact 45° angle on the disc sander. Check frequently while sanding to ensure that the opposite sides of the frame are identical as well as being, finally, of the required length. Precisely match the lengths of the top and bottom frame members to the width of the case as constructed; if the basic box is of plywood, remember to allow for the veneer thickness.

⑤ Apply glue to the door mitres and assemble the frame on a sheet of glass (exuded adhesive will have only a weak bond with the glass sheet, which will keep the frame perfectly flat). Check for squareness. If the mitres have been properly formed, the butt joints will be strong enough even for opening doors in cases made to the stated dimensions.

Break-arch Doors (Inverted Bell Top and Bell Top Cases)
⑥ Prepare the material for the stiles, bottom rail and top rail. Prepare the material for the planted glazing beads (the frame members are not rebated). The construction of this type of door is illustrated in Fig. 24. Note that the deep top rail is thinner than the other members, to allow the glass to pass behind it.

⑦ Cut the top and bottom rails about $\frac{1}{2}$ in (13 mm) longer than the finished size, then square the ends and bring

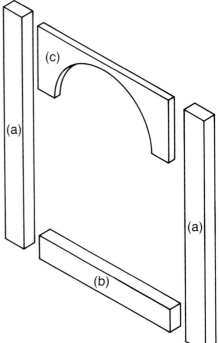

Fig 24 The break-arch door: (a) stiles; (b) bottom rail; (c) reduced-thickness top rail.

them to the correct length on the disc sander. Cut the arch in the top rail with the coping saw. Use abrasive paper wrapped around a bottle or canister to smooth the curved cut.

⑧ Cramp the stiles together in the vice and use a knife and try square to mark out the exact length. Part the pieces and extend the mark around each end.

⑨ Glue the door-frame members together, then lay them face down on a sheet of glass and check for squareness.

⑩ The curved glazing bead is formed by wrapping strips of veneer around a jar or tin of the same diameter as the arch (see Fig. 25). Using a knife and straight edge, cut the strips slightly wider than the finished size, to allow for sanding flat and square. Take the strips two-thirds of the way round the former, gluing them, one on top of the other, with PVA adhesive. Hold the ends down with masking tape.

Build up the thickness to match the straight glazing bead: about four layers will be required for the cases as detailed. Curved mouldings made in this way are quite rigid, and the former diameter needs to be exact or very slightly oversize.

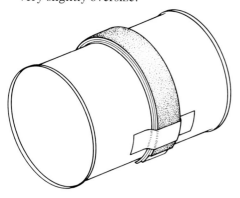

Fig 25 Wrap and glue strips of veneer around a jar or tin to form curved glazing beads.

⑪ Plane or disc-sand the stile ends down square and flush with the rails, then glue the glazing beads in position. Mitre the beads at internal angles and form butt joints at the junction between the arch beading and the two short lengths of top beading (see Fig. 71). The butt joints were found to be more satisfactory than mitres in this position but, if the case is scaled up in size, it would be preferable to form mitres at all six joints in the glazing bead.

Glazing the Doors
⑫ The doors are glazed with $\frac{1}{16}$ in or $\frac{5}{64}$ in (1.5 mm or 2 mm) thick picture glass (*not* the non-reflecting variety) after they have been stained and polished. The thinner glass is to be preferred for the smallest cases; larger cases should be glazed with the thicker material. The glass is held in position by glazing sprigs cut from the pointed ends of moulding pins. Use long-nosed pliers to push the sprigs into pre-formed holes in the stiles and rails.

Front Packing Pieces
⑬ Make the packing pieces which extend the top and bottom of the case outwards to the face of the door. Cut them slightly oversize, to allow for trimming. Even when the case is veneered, these packs are best made of the hardwood used for the mouldings.

⑭ Plane away any slight lipping at the joints in the case and sand it smooth. Locate the door frame on the case (do not glue it at this stage) and glue the packing pieces in position. Space them from the door with slips of folded paper to create an authentic gap.

Veneer and Mouldings
⑮ Plane the exposed sides and ends of

the packing pieces flush with the case, then lay the veneer to the sides and top if the construction is of plywood.

⑯ Prepare the mouldings for the case front and sides and glue them in position, as described earlier.

Dial Board and Rear Door
⑰ Cut out, and plane true and to fit, the dial board and the rear door. These two items are the same size and can be clamped together in the vice for planing.

⑱ Form the hole in the dial board for the movement spindle, together with any necessary sinking in the rear face for the body of the movement. Form pockets for any dummy hinges in the front door and for the true hinges in the rear door.

Feet, Spacing Strips and Door-stop Lath
⑲ Prepare, and glue in position, the feet, the spacing strips which separate the dial board from the front of the case, and the stop lath for the rear door.

Crown Moulding
⑳ Build up, and veneer if necessary, the moulding which crowns the case, making a generous allowance for waste in forming the deep mitres. Ensure that the base of the moulding is true and free from twist. It will rest on the sanding table when the mitres are being formed and any discrepancy will make it difficult to produce perfect joints.

㉑ Cut the prepared length of crown moulding into individual pieces on the mitre block, allowing $\frac{3}{4}$ in (19 mm) or more for waste on each piece. Sand the mitre cuts smooth, true, down to the correct size, and to a perfect 45° angle on the disc sander. Ensure that opposite sides are exactly equal in length.

㉒ Glue the pieces of crown moulding together, lay them on a sheet of glass and check for squareness. It may be necessary to hand-hold the assembly together until the glue grabs. In a warm room this takes between ten and fifteen minutes.

㉓ Prepare the capping piece and handle-fixing block, glue them in position and drill the holes for the handle bolts. Drill the holes in the top of the case for the screws which secure the crown-moulding assembly.

㉔ Place the crown moulding in position, mark the location of the screw holes with the awl, and drill thread holes in the moulding. Do a trial fixing to ensure that the moulding has been perfectly positioned, then remove it for finishing.

The top moulding is secured with screws in order to give access to the handle fixing nuts. If larger clocks are constructed and fitted with heavier, traditional movements, it would be preferable to extend the fixing bolts through to the inside of the case.

Final Items
㉕ Fix the rear door. Drill thread holes for the hook-and-eye catch.

The false door to the front is stained, polished and glazed before being glued in place. The crown moulding is also fixed after staining and polishing, and once the handle has been bolted in position.

Dial boards are retained by means of screws, driven a short way into the bottom and the top of the case, in the same manner as glazing sprigs (see Fig. 68).

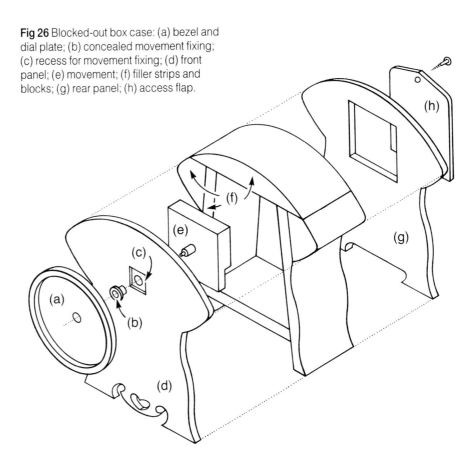

Fig 26 Blocked-out box case: (a) bezel and dial plate; (b) concealed movement fixing; (c) recess for movement fixing; (d) front panel; (e) movement; (f) filler strips and blocks; (g) rear panel; (h) access flap.

BLOCKED-OUT BOXES

This type of construction is adopted for cases with a flat front and back and a profile made up of pronounced curves. The Celtic-influence Art Nouveau case (Chapter Seventeen) is a typical example, and an 'exploded' view is given in Fig. 26. Assembly should proceed in the following stages.

Front and Back Panels
① Mark out the case front and back on a sheet of $\frac{3}{8}$ in (9 mm) plywood. Cut out the pieces with the coping saw, leaving a margin for finishing.

② Align the two pieces and temporarily fasten them together with moulding pins. Smooth convex curves on the disc sander and concave curves on the drum sander. Curves which are inaccessible to the machine must be smoothed with files and glasspaper. Part the two pieces when they have been finished to the required profile.

③ Form the hole for the movement spindle in the front panel and an external sinking if the fixing nut is to be located beneath the dial plate. Form any internal sinking to permit the movement spindle to project sufficiently. Cut the movement access hole in the back panel.

Blocking-out Pieces
④ Cut top, side, bottom and any blocking-out pieces from softwood strip thick enough to accommodate

the curvature of the sides. Disc-sand or plane the ends of the pieces to form accurate butt joints. Sand or plane the blocks to ensure a good fit with adjoining pieces.

Assembling the Box

⑤ Apply PVA adhesive and arrange the strips and blocks on the back panel, all projecting beyond the outline of the case. Glue the front panel in position, aligning it carefully with the back panel.

Shaping and Veneering

⑥ With the plywood front and back panels acting as templates, remove the projecting softwood, sawing away any large projections, then finishing the curving sides on the disc and drum sander. Again, any areas which cannot be reached by the machine will have to be cleaned up by hand.

⑦ Veneer the case. Specific guidance on laying veneer on the Celtic-influence Art Nouveau case is given in Chapter Two.

Final Items

⑧ Make the rear-access cover flap. Mark the position of the dial-plate fixing screws and the cover-flap screw, and drill thread holes.

Using This Construction Technique for Other Cases

This form of construction can be adopted for the balloon, lancet top, arch top and Napoleon-style cases (Chapters Eleven, Twelve and Eighteen). Indeed, if these cases are made much larger than the ones detailed in later chapters, blocked-out-box is preferable to solid-block construction, as the risk of drying shrinkage and cracking becomes greater as block size increases.

When sharp curves are involved,

the grain of the side veneer must run from front to back. However, veneer grain is traditionally orientated the opposite way and this arrangement should be adopted if the curves are gentle enough (e.g. the lancet top, Napoleon-style clock and larger versions of the balloon clock).

SOLID-BLOCK CASES

This type of case is depicted in Fig. 27. Either one-piece or built-up blocks can be used. Built-up blocks are more economical in the use of timber, as they can be assembled roughly to the profile of the clock, and it is easier to cut the chamber for

the movement if the case is in two halves. The arch top, lancet top, balloon and chamfer top cases were formed from built-up blocks. The Napoleon-style case was made in one piece. Construction should proceed as follows.

Forming and Shaping the Block

① If a built-up block is being used, cut the individual pieces from the same length of wood and plane them true and square, paying particular attention to the faces which are to be glued together. Mark out and form the movement chamber: make two straight saw cuts and remove waste wood with a chisel, as if forming a

Fig 27 Solid-block case: (a) bezel and dial plate; (b) concealed movement fixing; (c) movement-mounting strip; (d) movement; (e) solid-block case; (f) access flap; (g) base mouldings; (h) feet.

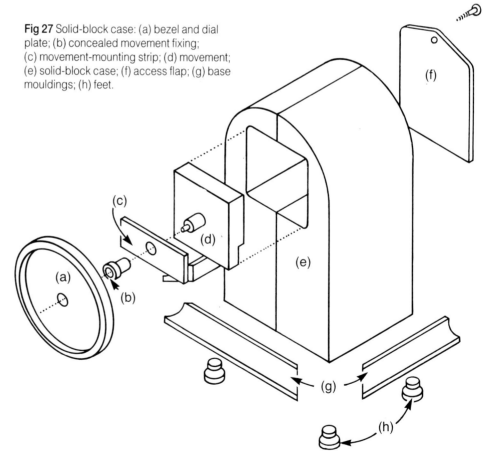

Fig 28 Pieces of a built-up block for the balloon case.

halving joint (see Fig. 28). Glue and tightly cramp the pieces together.

② Mark out the profile of the case on the block: the setting-out board described in Chapter Four will be needed for the balloon and Napoleon clocks (see Fig. 30). If a one-piece block is being used, it is best to form the movement chamber before the case is cut out, as the greater area of wood will reduce the chance of splitting. Drill $\frac{1}{4}$ in (6 mm) holes just inside each corner of the marked-out chamber, to allow the saw blade to enter the block and turn.

③ Cut out the clock. If a bow saw or mechanical band saw is not available, remove material from convex curves with a series of straight cuts, then drill a row of connecting holes to form the cuts for concave curves (e.g. the waist of the balloon clock). A $\frac{3}{8}$ in (9 mm) drill is about right for this purpose. Keep these rough cuts a safe distance away from the marked-out profile of the clock: an inclined drill or saw can easily stray into the body of the case. What constitutes a safe distance will

vary from worker to worker, but $\frac{3}{8}$ in (9 mm) is suggested as a minimum for cases $2\frac{1}{2}$ in (63 mm) or more deep. All of the solid-block cases were cut out in this way.

④ Use the disc sander to finish convex curves and the drum sander for concave areas. The combination machine removes material quickly and the rough-cut cases can be brought to the correct profile in a few minutes. A great deal of dust is produced and a face mask should be worn during this operation. Plane the front and back faces flat, true and parallel.

Mouldings and Turnings
⑤ Prepare the mouldings, turnings and any other surface-fixed parts and glue them in position. This process is described in detail earlier in the chapter.

Concealed Movement Fixing
⑥ If the movement mounting nut is to be hidden behind the dial, cut a 1 in (25 mm) wide strip of $\frac{3}{8}$ in (9 mm) plywood and trim it to a tight fit

across the movement chamber. Apply adhesive, then locate the strip just deep enough inside the chamber to accommodate the thickness of the movement fixing nut beneath the dial back plate. Fig. 39 makes the arrangement clear.

Final Items
⑦ Make the rear cover flap for the movement chamber. Mark the position of the dial-plate fixing screws and the cover-flap screw and drill thread holes.

FINIAL BLOCKS

A swept finial has to be cut and shaped for the pendule d'officier case (Chapter Fourteen) and this decoration is optional for the balloon and arch top clocks.

Cut a block and plane it true, square and down to the overall size of the finial. Mark the finial front profile on the face of the block, then saw and carve it to the required shape. Mark the side profile on one of the now curved sides of the block, and saw and carve it as before. Wrap abrasive paper around a cylindrical former for the final smoothing process.

The base of the finial for balloon and arch top clocks has to be given a concave curve to match the profile of the case. Saw and carve the base as closely as possible to the required shape, then wrap a strip of abrasive paper over the crown of the clock case and use this to grind the finial base down to an exact fit.

8 clear, high-gloss polyurethane varnish (for the Art Deco clock, Chapter Nineteen, only)

9 clear, matt polyurethane varnish

10 oil-based white undercoat (for the painted Art Nouveau case, Chapter Seventeen, only)

11 methylated spirits (methyl alcohol in America): used as a thinner and brush-cleaner for french polishes

12 white spirit (mineral spirit or Stoddard solvent in America): used as a thinner and brush-cleaner for the wood dyes, varnish and paint

13 steel wool, 0000 grade

14 wet and dry abrasive paper, 400 grade (the finest)

15 stencil card

16 masking tape

17 artists' acrylic colours: titanium white and ivory black for simulating inlay; the following additional colours are required for decorating the Egyptian revival (Chapter Thirteen) and Art Nouveau cases and the moon dial – quinacridone red, red iron oxide, azo yellow light, cobalt blue and ultramarine blue, all by Winsor and Newton

18 sundry small jars and containers for paint-mixing

19 clear cellulose, cellulose thinners and cellulose-based balsa cement: used for dial-making and finishing (see Chapters Five and Six)

20 draughtsman's tracing paper

21 green baize or felt for furniture-protecting pads for the clock feet

Notes on the Above Items

The plastic-wood-type stopping (1) must accept wood dyes and not ghost through the finish as a lighter or darker patch. Most stoppings of this kind are satisfactory, but check on scrap wood before using.

Fillers (2), wood dyes (4) and polishes (5, 6 and 7) should preferably all be purchased from one reputable supplier. The solvent most commonly used for the wood dyes or stains retailed to small users is white spirit (12), and the guidance given here assumes the use of a product of this kind. Applied in accordance with the manufacturer's instructions, consistently good results are assured. Other types of stain, including traditional stains which have a chemical action on the wood, are available from craft suppliers. These stains generally call for more skill and expertise in their application.

Button polish (5) was applied to almost all of the cases. It has a very long shelf-life and takes its name from the button-shaped discs of lac formed during refining. Its translucent, golden-brown colour softens any coldness or harshness in the wood dyes. Much used by restorers, it imparts a rich, antique finish to the clocks.

The bleaching of the lac to make white polish changes its chemical structure. After a shelf-life of about eighteen months, polish made from bleached lac becomes very slow-drying, producing a gummy surface which refuses to harden. Buy white polish of a reputable make only, and from outlets with a good turnover. Even then apply two or three coats to scrap wood to check that it will dry before applying it to a clock case.

Decoration is stencilled on to the Art Nouveau cases. Traditional stencil sheet is produced by treating manila card with linseed oil. Modern exponents of the craft, which is undergoing something of a revival, use acetate or other plastic film. Stencils for the clock cases were cut from translucent high-impact polystyrene sheet. This material is sold in model shops as Plastic Building Card. It cuts well, offering just the right amount of resistance to the knife, does not tear and designs can be traced through it. It should *not* be used with cellulose paints as the solvent dissolves it.

Artists' acrylic colours (17) were used to decorate the cases. These highly refined emulsion paints were chosen because of their opacity at consistencies which will flow in the ruling pens, and because of their drying characteristics. Manufacturers give different names to very similar colours. If difficulty is encountered in obtaining the quinacridone red and azo yellow light, for example, try alizarin crimson and cadmium yellow light.

TECHNIQUES: GENERAL GUIDANCE

Whether or not the cases are stained, and if they are, what colour, are matters of personal preference. A desire to match other furniture, to give wood an appearance of age or to make wood take on the rich colour it is traditionally supposed to have – these are all common motivators.

The natural colour and, more particularly, the porosity of the wood have a great effect on the final result. The same stain will produce a much darker finish on a porous sample of a timber than on a more impervious piece. Filling the grain of the wood and the type of polish used also have subtle but significant effects. Wood stains or dyes from any one manufacturer's range can be mixed to produce a variety of shades, and they can be made less intense by the addition of white spirit.

Apply french polish and varnish in a warm, dry room; never in a cold, damp atmosphere. If possible, remove the cases to another room for rubbing down and dusting off, so as to avoid any contamination of the polishing area.

Take some time to experiment on fairly large – at least 3 × 3 in (75 × 75 mm) – scrap pieces of the wood actually used for the case. Go through the whole process – initial sanding, grainfilling if adopted, staining and polishing – before making a choice.

THE FINISHING PROCESS: FRENCH POLISHING AND SIMULATING BOXWOOD INLAY

The lines which simulate stringing or inlay have to be ruled during the french-polishing process. The entire procedure is as follows.

Preparation
① Check the case thoroughly for blemishes. Try removing any minor dents by damping the surface and applying a hot clothes-iron through sheets of paper until the area dries. Gently scrape and glasspaper away any glue residues; if left, they will ghost through the finish as light patches. Make good any tiny surface defects with plastic wood. Use flour-grade glasspaper to give the bare wood a final smoothing, taking care to clean up and sharpen, not blur, the detail of the mouldings.

Filling the Grain
② If the wood is open-grained and a mirror-like shine is required, the application of filler will avoid the need to brush on, then rub down, an excessive number of coats of polish. The filler must be coloured to match the wood, and some manufacturers recommend thinning and tinting it with their wood dye. The paste filler is applied with a rag, rubbing hard across the grain, until the pores are

filled. Surplus material is then wiped off and the case left overnight to dry.

Four or five of the mahogany cases were treated in this way, and the process did make it easier to obtain a good finish.

Staining the Wood
③ Ensure that the case is free of dust, paying particular attention to clearing grooves in the mouldings, then apply the wood dye, liberally and evenly, with a brush. If this highlights any patches of glue which have been missed, scrape them off as quickly as possible and brush more dye over the disturbed areas.

Leave the case to take up the dye, then wipe away any residue with a lint-free cloth. If a less intense effect is required, wipe the case before all of the dye has been absorbed into the wood. Allow the case to dry out thoroughly overnight.

Polishing: The First Stages
④ Brush the case free of dust and loose fibres. Pour a little button polish into a dish and, using the artist's wash brush, apply an even coat to the case, one face at a time, taking care to avoid runs and ridges at corners. Flow the polish on and brush it out in one direction only. The solvent evaporates quickly, so keep brushing to a minimum and do not disturb areas which have begun to harden.

⑤ Apply a further two coats of polish, allowing each one to harden before applying the next. Work quickly to avoid disturbing earlier coats. Avoid splashes and runs: these will soften and deeply mark the built-up finish, which will then have to be cut back almost to the wood. Leave the case in a warm, dry atmosphere while the polish hardens thoroughly.

⑥ Remove any blemishes from the surface of the polish with 0000-grade steel wool. Work carefully. It is easy to cut down to the wood, especially at corners. If this happens, apply more dye to the bared areas and allow it to dry before proceeding.

⑦ Brush on a further two coats of button polish. The case should now be beginning to look presentable. When the fifth coat has thoroughly hardened, lightly smooth it with steel wool to remove any blemishes and to produce a matt surface ready to take the ruled lines which simulate inlay.

Simulating Inlay and Applying Decoration: Marking Out
⑧ Mount cases with curved sides on the setting-out board (see Fig. 30) and locate the exact compass-point positions by a mixture of measurement and trial and error. Fix the pencil attachment, with a soft lead, in the compasses and faintly mark out the curved lines on the case. Mark out the straight lines with a straight edge and soft pencil.

Using the Ruling Pens
⑨ Squeeze a little titanium white acrylic colour into a shallow dish and add water until it has a creamy consistency. Fit the ruling-pen attachment into the compasses, use the No. 2 artist's brush to load it with colour, then check for opacity, flow and line width on a scrap piece of wood. Fill the pen to about $\frac{1}{4}$ in (6 mm) above the tip before beginning to draw: it is almost impossible to make clean joins if the pen runs out mid-line. Start the flow by drawing the pen across the back of the hand. After the curved lines have been drawn and the colour has dried, use the ruling pen and straight edge to draw the straight lines.

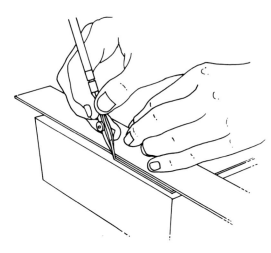

Fig 31 Ruling lines on a case to simulate boxwood or ebony inlay.

Line width is controlled by the knurled screw, which sets the distance between the pen blades. Constructors who have not used one of these pens should practise on scrap wood before attempting to rule lines on a finished clock. Hold the pen vertically, or at a slight trailing angle, and clean the blades after drawing each line. The acrylic colour dries quickly and the pens will not draw if they are dirty. Figs. 30 and 31 show the compasses and ruling pen being used to simulate inlay.

Lines should be a heavy $\frac{1}{32}$ in (or 1 mm) wide for cases built to the recommended sizes, and they should be located a tight $\frac{1}{4}$ in (6 mm) in from the panel edge. If wider lines are required for larger cases, it is best to draw two lines side by side. Real boxwood and ebony lines are sold in about eight sizes, from $\frac{3}{64}$ in to $\frac{1}{4}$ in (1 mm to 6 mm) wide. Even on the largest versions of the cases, the lines ought not to be wider than about $\frac{1}{16}$ in (1.5 mm).

The decorations to the lancet clock (Chapter Twelve) and the incised

corners to some of the simulated stringing call for curves of small radius. Use the spring bows for these.

Ruling Lines on Swept Finials

⑩ Guides for drawing lines on swept finials (e.g. the pendule d'officier clock, Chapter Fourteen) can be made from stout card. Press the card against the concave finial, mark the profile with a sharp pencil and then cut the card along this line to produce a template of the correct shape (see Fig. 32). A strip of card glued beneath the template will lift it off the surface and prevent colour flowing under it.

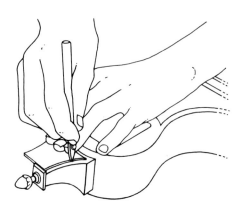

Fig 32 Using a card template to rule lines on a concave finial.

Making Corrections

⑪ Mistakes can be corrected by very gently scraping away the acrylic colour with a scalpel blade as soon as the initial drying has taken place (after one or two minutes in a warm room). At this stage the paint is soft and rubbery and can be removed without marking the polish if care is taken. When the paint has completely hardened, its adhesion is strong and removal is therefore more difficult.

Applying Decoration

⑫ Stencilled decoration designed to imitate marquetry (e.g. the Celtic-influence Art Nouveau case, Chapter Seventeen) is also applied at this stage. Stencilling is dealt with later in this chapter. Brightly coloured decoration must be applied *after* the white lining has been glazed to a boxwood shade; otherwise the colours will be dulled by the button polish.

Glazing the White Lines

⑬ Apply three more coats of button polish, making eight in all. This will glaze the white lines to a yellowish-brown and should bring the case to a state of completion. If the finish is still not quite satisfactory, very gently rub the case down with 0000-grade steel wool and apply further coats of polish, thinned with a little methylated spirit. A substantial body of shellac will have built up on the case by this stage and hardening times between coats may increase. Do not attempt to handle the case unless the finish is thoroughly hard.

Velvet Sheen Finish

⑭ If a velvet sheen is preferred, rub the case very gently in the direction of the grain using 0000-grade wire wool lubricated with wax polish. This must be carried out as a final treatment, after the protective glaze has been applied to any coloured decorations (see next section).

APPLYING COLOURED DECORATIONS TO THE EGYPTIAN REVIVAL CLOCK

Pens are used to apply the brightly coloured decorations to the Egyptian revival case. The procedure is as follows.

Preparing the Surface

① Very gently matt down the front of the case with 0000-grade steel wool, taking care not to disturb the glaze over the lines.

Marking Out

② Mark out the spacings for the frieze decorations on the edge of a sheet of paper, and cut off a $\frac{3}{32}$ in (2 mm) wide strip and attach it to the case, just above the roll moulding, with tiny pieces of masking tape. Rest a $\frac{3}{8}$ in (9 mm) wide, square-ended strip of thin Perspex (acrylic) sheet against the roll to act as a set square, then rule on the decorations, one colour at a time (see Fig. 33). Adjust the pen to produce a reasonably fine line – say, $\frac{1}{32}$ in (0.7 mm) wide – and draw the outlines of the rectangles, which can then be filled in with the No. 2 brush.

Transferring the Design to the Case

③ Trace the full-size pattern given in Chapter Thirteen (Fig. 94), then use carbon paper and a hard, sharp pencil to transfer it to the case. Mark the centres of the circles.

Some distortion will arise when the design is transferred. Using a sharp, soft pencil, draw faint guidelines through the tops of the lotus flowers, the centres of the circles, the cross-members, etc., to aid the correct ruling in of the design with the pen. Details of the construction of the pattern are also given in Chapter Thirteen (see Fig. 95), both to guide setting out and to facilitate enlargement, should this be required.

Drawing in the Design

④ Using the ruling pen and a small 60° set square held against the top of the plinth, draw in the pattern, one colour at a time. The small spring-bow compasses will be required for the circles and the lotus buds. Again, the No. 2 brush is used to block in areas of solid colour. A deep-blue, light-blue and reddish-brown combination, typical of schemes adopted by the ancient Egyptians, was chosen and the actual colours used are listed below:

deep-blue areas:	cobalt blue
light-blue areas:	cobalt blue and titanium white
reddish-brown areas:	red iron oxide with a touch of azo yellow light

A fine, light-blue line was ruled around the areas of deep blue and brown in order to improve contrast with the dark, mahogany case. If a lighter wood is used, this will not be necessary.

Protective Coating

⑤ When the acrylic colours have hardened, protect and seal them by applying two coats of white french polish to the front of the case. This dries clear and will not dull the brilliance of the decorations.

Ruling the pattern on the case calls for a steady hand and some patience, but the final effect is striking and well worth the effort. The finished clock is shown in the photograph on page 107.

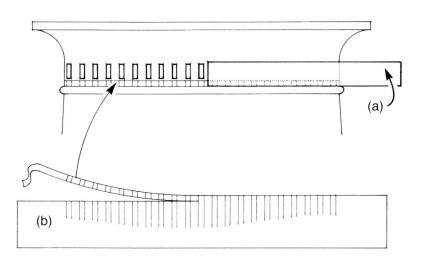

Fig 33 Ruling decoration on the gorge of the Egyptian revival clock: (a) strip of Perspex used as a set square; (b) strip of paper.

APPLYING PAINT FINISHES

The Art Nouveau case in the manner of the Glasgow Four is painted and stencilled. The paint finish should be applied in the following way.

Preparation

① Make good any remaining slight defects in the case with plastic wood and smooth with flour-grade glasspaper.

② Brush dust from the case and apply two coats of button polish, slightly thinned with methylated spirit, to act as a sanding-sealer. Smooth with flour-grade glasspaper.

Painting: The First Stages

③ Thin the oil-based white undercoat with white spirit until it flows easily and does not hold brush marks. Remove any gritty particles by straining the paint through fine nylon mesh, then apply the paint in thin, even coats. About four coats will be required to obliterate the wood and develop a good surface. Allow overnight drying between coats.

④ Smooth the above finish with 400-grade wet and dry abrasive paper, using slightly soapy water as a lubricant.

⑤ If the rubbing down results in the wood ghosting through, apply more coats of thinned undercoat and repeat the process until a perfect surface has been prepared.

Painting: The Final Stages

⑥ Drop by drop, add very small amounts of yellow, black and brown oil-based paint to the thinned undercoat to kill the white and produce a pale-ivory colour. Experiment with a small jar of paint to get the proportions right. Any type of oil-based paint will do for tinting, from artists' oil colours to scraps left over from domestic painting jobs.

⑦ Apply a coat of the ivory paint, allow it to dry and check the shade (it will probably darken on drying). Adjust the colour as necessary by adding more white or more tints, then apply two or three more coats. Smooth the finish with 400-grade wet and dry, as before, and a perfect, porcelain-like surface will result.

⑧ Stencil on the decoration using artists' acrylic colours. Details of the stencilling technique are given in the section below.

Protective Coating

⑨ Apply two coats of matt, polyurethane varnish to seal and protect the decoration and give a harder-wearing surface to the case.

STENCILLING

The Art Nouveau-style cases have stencilled decoration, and full-size patterns are included in Chapter Seventeen. The procedure is as follows.

Preparing the Stencil

① Use tracing paper to transfer the design to traditional, opaque stencil card. If plastic film is being used, the design can be traced direct.

② Cut out the pattern with a sharp, pointed knife. If mistakes are made, stick adhesive tape over the area and cut again. Only half of the pattern needs to be cut out for the Celtic-influence case, the stencil being turned over to produce the other half. Quite apart from the saving of effort, this ensures perfect symmetry.

③ Locate the stencil on the case and hold it in position with masking tape.

Mixing and Applying the Colours

④ Only small quantities of colour are required, but mix sufficient to do the whole job, as it is difficult to duplicate subtle shades exactly. Add little or no water: if the colour does not have a stiff consistency, it will tend to flow beneath the stencil.

⑤ Dip the stencil brush in the colour and dab it on a sheet of paper to remove any surplus. The brush must be lightly loaded.

⑥ Apply three or four coats of colour and allow each coat to dry between applications (between one and two minutes).

Cleaning Up the Design and Painting Out Ties

⑦ Use the curved-blade scalpel very gently to scrape away any areas of unwanted colour. Use the No. 2 artist's brush to paint out the stencil ties on the Celtic-influence clock and for any cleaning up and corrections.

Do not paint out the ties on the ivory-coloured Art Nouveau clock and resist any temptation to sharpen up the outline: stencilling was a distinctive feature of the work of the Glasgow Four.

Colour Mixes

The various colour mixes used for the designs are scheduled opposite.

MARQUETRY TECHNIQUES

Great skill would be required to produce a marquetry version of the slender, flowing design on the Celtic-influence Art Nouveau case, although virtuosos of the craft may still wish to try. Marquetry techniques and

CELTIC-INFLUENCE CASE

A pale, yellowish-buff, made by tinting white with a dash of azo yellow light and a hint of red iron oxide. The white was tinted in this instance in order to produce a slightly deeper shade than would have been achieved by just the three coats of button polish glaze alone. The final effect is shown in the photograph on page 139.

SCOTTISH-INFLUENCE CASE

Rose blossoms: pink, made by tinting titanium white with quinacridone red; hints of ultramarine blue and ivory black were added to produce a more subtle shade.

Seed pods and dial: mauve or violet, made by mixing quinacridone red, ultramarine blue and white; again, a touch of ivory black was added to remove the harshness from the colour.

Leaves and stems: green, made by mixing azo yellow light, ultramarine blue and a touch of black.

The stencils used for applying decoration to the Art Nouveau clocks, and the marquetry decoration ready for laying on the Art Deco case. (The pointed scalpel blade is ideal for cutting out stencils and marquetry, and the rounded blade is useful for gently scraping away any unwanted areas of paint)

commercially dyed wood veneers were, however, used to produce the bold, geometric design on the Art Deco case (Chapter Nineteen). The procedure is as follows.

Cutting Out the Design

① Trace the full-size pattern reproduced in Chapter Nineteen. Note that the design extends behind the plinth to the bottom of the case.

② Cut out the harewood veneer for the front of the case. Cut out a piece of crimson and a piece of black veneer, each large enough to cover the entire design.

③ Mark the centre line on the harewood veneer with a soft pencil. Stack the three pieces of veneer on a cutting board: black, red, then harewood uppermost. Secure all four edges of each piece to the board with masking tape. Position the traced pattern on the harewood, using the centre line as a guide. Secure the pattern with masking tape.

④ Using a sharp knife and straight edge, cut along the outer profile of the pattern, where red adjoins grey, gradually slicing through all three sheets. Do not disturb the stack of sheets and the traced pattern. If necessary, apply more masking tape to the pattern to hold it in place.

⑤ Cut along the inner lines of the pattern, where black meets red.

Assembling and Laying the Marquetry

⑥ Gently untape the three sheets of veneer from the cutting board, discard unwanted pieces and assemble the pattern, holding it together with masking tape applied to the front face.

⑦ Draw a centre line on the case to aid the accurate alignment of the marquetry. Apply contact adhesive to veneer and case front, and lay the veneer when it is touch-dry.

Use of Natural Veneers

Natural wood can be substituted for the coloured veneers. Padauk is the brightest red wood available, but it is not as vivid as the chemically treated material. Try Macassar ebony for the black areas: this is a dark-brown veneer. Gaboon ebony, which is the black variety, is not converted into knife-cut veneer.

Do not use white-spirit-based wood dyes to colour marquetry veneers. Varnish or french polish will make them bleed.

GLOSS VARNISH FINISH

A lacquered finish was considered appropriate for the Jazz Age, Art Deco case. The procedure is as follows.

① Apply two coats of clear, gloss, polyurethane varnish to the case, then gently rub down with 0000-grade steel wool. Use a good-quality brush to apply the varnish and allow overnight drying, in a warm room, between coats.

② Apply a further two coats of varnish, rubbing down after each one, then apply the final coat, making five in all.

EBONIZING

The pedimented architectural case (Chapter Eight) is completely ebonized, and ebonized bands decorate the dome-topped Renaissance clock (Chapter Seven).

Forming Ebonized Bands

Do *not* use spirit-based ebony wood dye to stain veneer to form the bands. Solvents in the polish will make it bleed over adjoining areas.

The dado and frieze on the Renaissance clock are ebonized by applying ivory black artists' acrylic colour after the final polishing of the case. Two or three coats of thinned colour build up to a velvet black which requires no further finishing. If difficulty is experienced in cutting-in to the mouldings which border the bands, use the ruling pen to draw a perfect edge.

Ebonizing a Complete Case

Spirit-based ebony wood dye is used to stain the architectural case. This case is completely black, so bleeding is not a problem. After staining, the case is button-polished, in the manner already described.

Ghosting through of the groundwork is a problem with ebony dye or stain. Professional polishers overcome this by using black french polish, which is available from some of the suppliers of wood and finishing materials who advertise in woodworking and craft magazines. The use of this material is strongly recommended.

Rubbing the finished case, in the direction of the grain, with 0000-grade steel wool lubricated with wax polish will impart a more authentic, duller sheen.

PROTECTING POLISHED SURFACES

When the finishing process is complete, glue $\frac{1}{2}$ in (13 mm) diameter discs of green baize or felt to the underside of the feet to act as furniture protectors. White PVA adhesive is a suitable glue.

CHAPTER FIVE

Movements and Other Clock Parts

SUPPLIERS

Suppliers of movements, bezels, dials, insertion units, hands, pendulums and decorative brassware advertise widely in woodworking and craft magazines. As they tend to specialize, it is a good idea to obtain catalogues from a number of them. Clock movements and accessories can also be obtained from many of the veneer and hardwood suppliers, who also advertise in these magazines.

QUARTZ MOVEMENTS

The design of domestic quartz movements is fairly standardized, but the method of fixing adopted in America differs from that used in Europe. Fig. 34 illustrates this. In America, the hand-drive spindles pass through a threaded bush and a nut is used to secure the movement. In Europe, the spindles pass through a tubular bolt which engages with threads in the case.

Junghans 738 movements, illustrated in Fig. 35, were fitted in most of the clocks. Some of these basic movements have snap-on access covers. Always hold these covers in place while pushing the hour hand on to its shaft; otherwise the movement may burst open.

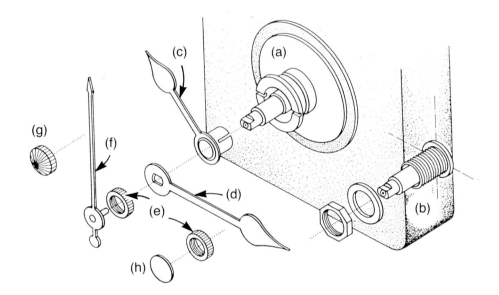

A version which chimes on the hour is available as the 738 Westminster. Here the critical dimensions are unchanged, but the case depth is increased, from $\frac{5}{8}$ in (16 mm) to 1 in (25 mm). This unit can be used to provide a chiming facility in solid-block cases which have small movement chambers (e.g. the balloon clock, Chapter Eleven).

The basic 717 pendulum movement and the hour-chiming 717 Westminster version are illustrated in Fig. 36. One or other of these movements was installed in the pendulum clocks. The swing of the purely decorative pendulums is not

Fig 34 Quartz movement and hand fixings; (a) European tubular bolt fixing; (b) American threaded bush and nut fixing; (c) hour hand with split collet; (d) minute hand with 'I' slot; (e) open hand fixing nut; (f) second hand; (g) blind hand fixing nut used when second hand omitted; (h) paper disc and open nut used as an alternative to a blind nut.

SQUARE AND STEEPLE DIALS

The picture-mount technique can also be used to make square or steeple dials when only a round dial is available. This is illustrated in Fig. 44. Use ivory or white mounting card if the process is just being used to produce a dial of different shape.

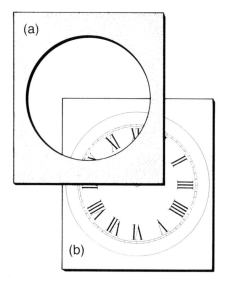

Fig 44 Using mounting card to convert a round dial into a rectangular or steeple-topped dial: (a) window in mounting card; (b) dial stuck to backing card.

COLOURED DIALS

Coloured dials are fitted to the Egyptian revival, Glasgow Four-influence Art Nouveau and Art Deco clocks pictured in the photographs on pages 107, 139 and 150.

Coloured Backing Discs

Discs of coloured mounting card can be used for the backing, or stout card can be painted with artists' acrylic colour. This last method is appropriate for the Egyptian revival and Art Nouveau clocks (Chapters Thirteen and Seventeen), where a close colour match with the case decorations is desirable.

Brass Hour Markers

Cut hour markers for the Egyptian revival clock from a $\frac{1}{4}$ in (6 mm) wide strip of brass. Using a try square, mark out $\frac{1}{8}$ in (3 mm) lengths along the strip and snip them off with metal cutters or sharp scissors. Cut about eighteen, then select the twelve which are best matched. Place the markers individually between smooth metal plates, then flatten out any curling in a vice or by hammering. Polish them to a brilliant shine. Triangular markers are required for the Art Deco clock (Chapter Nineteen). They are made in a similar way.

Fixing the Markers

Mark out the dial plate very faintly with a soft pencil, as shown in Fig. 93. De-grease the markers by dipping them in methylated spirit (methyl alcohol in America), dry them off, apply a smear of cyanoacrylate adhesive (super glue) and press them into position on the dial. Tweezers will be needed for this. Using the No. 2 artist's brush, carefully apply clear cellulose to the brass to seal in the shine.

White Hour Markers

White zeros from sheets of dry transfer lettering are rubbed down to form hour markers on the Art Nouveau clock dial. The centres of the zeros are filled in with white acrylic colour applied with the No. 2 artist's brush.

DIAL NUMERALS

The popularity of Roman numerals has endured from the birth of clock-making to the present day. They have been used to mark the dials of clocks constructed in every style, including Art Nouveau and Art Deco, and are to be preferred for most of the clocks in this collection.

Arabic numerals were used more frequently towards the close of the nineteenth century and were the norm for Arts and Crafts Movement clocks. However, even such ardent followers of the Movement as Charles Voysey sometimes reverted to traditional practice, and an interesting wooden dial, attributed to Herbert Horne, which is painted with the sun and signs of the zodiac, has Roman numerals. This $12\frac{1}{4}$ in (306 mm) diameter dial is in the care of the William Morris Gallery, Walthamstow.

HANDS

The various styles of hands fitted to the clocks are illustrated in Fig. 45. They represent a compromise between authenticity and ready availability, and the colour plates and drawings indiate the most appropriate choices for particular clocks. American suppliers list other styles which are particularly suitable for traditional American timepieces.

Minute hands fitted to quartz movements have a narrow pivot slot (there is usually a square hole in traditional movement hands) and are known in America as 'I' shaft hands.

Hand Finish

Black hands should be used with white dials and silver-effect chapter rings. Brass hands should be used with coloured dials and the pierced-brass chapter ring fitted to the Arts and Crafts clock (Chapter Sixteen). The spade hands on the Glasgow Four-influence Art Nouveau clock are painted ivory to match the case.

The second hand on the Art Deco clock is painted red.

Second Hands

Centre second hands were not normally fitted to spring- or weight-driven domestic clocks, and they have accordingly been confined to the pendule d'officier and the glass-fronted carriage clocks (Chapter Fourteen) and the Art Deco clock (Chapter Nineteen). Pendules d'officier have a slender, additional hand for alarm setting, and this feature is sometimes found on carriage clocks. A second hand does not, therefore, look too out of place on these timepieces.

Hand Size

The size of a pair of clock hands is the length of the minute hand, measured from pivot to tip. The sweep of the second hand is measured in the same way. Ideally, the tip of the minute hand should just reach the outer edge of the time ring on the dial.

Modifying Hands

The inexpensive hands supplied for use with quarts movements are generally manufactured by a photo-etch process. If the minute hand is a little too long, the tip can be removed with a sharp knife and, where necessary, the point restored by scraping and sanding the sides. A

touch of black acrylic colour will make good any exposure of bright metal.

This technique was used to reduce $1\frac{5}{8}$ in (41 mm) spade hands to $1\frac{1}{2}$ in (38 mm) to suit the 3 in (75 mm) dials used on many of the clocks. The tip of these hands is a thin filament of metal deliberately made long enough for trimming, and no repointing is necessary.

Fixing Hands

Hand-fixing arrangements are depicted in Fig. 34. If difficulty is encountered in pressing the hour hand on to its shaft, insert the blade of a small screwdriver into the split in the collet and gently widen it. Never use excessive force to drive the hour hand home.

Minute hands are held in place by a knurled nut. Blind nuts are available for use when second hands are not fitted, but a more authentic look can be achieved by closing an open nut with a disc of paper and applying black acrylic colour to the disc. Produce the discs by inserting self-adhesive labels into a standard office punch. The alternative methods are depicted in the figure and the various photographs.

Fix the hands with the movement set at 12 o'clock. If a chiming unit is being fitted, insert a battery to ensure that the hand setting is synchronized with the chimes. Minute-hand slots are usually a loose fit, and some fine adjustments may be necessary to

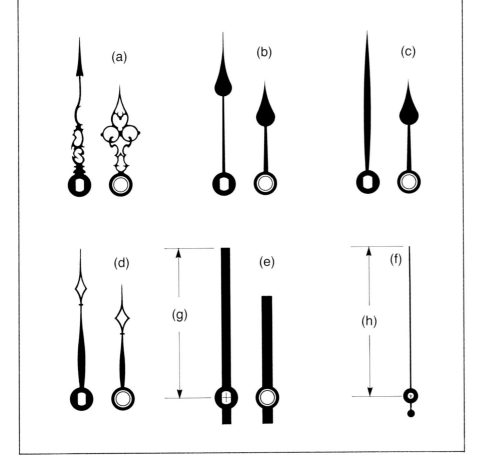

Fig 45 Hand styles chosen for the clocks: (a) serpentine; (b) spade; (c) finger and spade; (d) cathedral; (e) baton; (f) a second hand. The size of a pair of hands is the length, pivot to tip (g), of the minute hand. This is also the method (h) of sizing second hands.

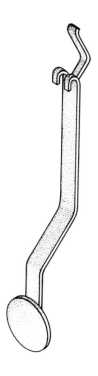

Fig 46 Cranked pendulum rod fitted to movement in the American clocks to bring the bob close to the glass front panel. The vertical metal tag above the suspension is bent to press forward against the cradle on the movement and keep the bob in its forward position.

match the onset of chiming precisely with hour location. Minute hands may also need gently curving towards the dial to prevent them chafing against the glass.

PENDULUMS

Commercial Units

The pendulum drive power developed by standard quartz units is limited, and lightweight bobs pressed from thin sheet brass are normally supplied. Bob diameters range from $1\frac{7}{8}$ in to $3\frac{1}{2}$ in (47 mm to 89 mm) for standard units, and up to $5\frac{1}{2}$ in (140 mm) diameter for the more powerful quartz long case clock movements. Some American retailers carry the full range of sizes; choice is more limited in the United Kingdom.

The smaller bobs are usually a sliding fit on a $\frac{3}{16}$ in (5 mm) brass suspension rod, which is cut to the required length, one end being bent to hook over a cradle on the movement.

Pendulums for the American Clocks

The 1 in (25 mm) diameter pendulum bobs for the scaled-down American clocks are cut from thin sheet brass. After polishing, the bobs and the suspension rods are brushed with clear cellulose. They can then be stuck together with balsa cement. These bobs have to swing just behind the glass, and Fig. 46 shows how to cut and form the rod in order to ensure this happens.

DECORATIVE BRASSWARE AND HANDLES

Brass feet, lion's heads, cherub and scroll spandrels, lifting rings, handles and decorative finials are required for the clocks. Dimensions and a description of the various items of

brassware are given in the components lists, and this, together with the figures and colour photographs in this book, should enable constructors to identify and obtain suitable parts.

Using Cabinet Fittings

Reproduction antique cabinet fittings can often be used for clock cases. The handles on the carriage clocks (Chapter Fourteen) and the lifting rings on the chamfer top clock (Chapter Thirteen) are brass drawer pulls. Handles can usually be separated from unwanted back plates and the pivot stems bolted directly to the clock case.

Antiquing Brassware

Sometimes it is desirable to impart a patina of age to new brassware. The traditional method of doing this is to treat the item with tourmaline black (note, though, that this is a poisonous chemical). After the desired depth of patina has been achieved, the item is washed and dried, and the finish fixed with jade oil.

An alternative method involves the application of tinted, matt poly-urethane varnish to the metal. Pour a small quantity of varnish into a container and add tiny amounts of wood dye or stain. Try one part red mahogany to two parts ebony to four parts dark oak stain to twelve parts varnish as a basis for experiment, adjusting the proportions until the desired antique effect is obtained.

The bezel of the round dial carriage clock (see photograph on page 121) was antiqued by this process to make it match the handle.

Some clock bezels are pressed from anodized aluminium. Do not apply tourmaline to these.

CHAPTER SIX

Constructing a Moon Dial

Moon dials were often fitted in the arches of inverted bell top and bell top clocks, but they can be purchased only as integral parts of large, long-case clock dials. They add colour and interest, and this chapter is devoted to the construction of a dial and mechanism that can be accommodated in smaller cases. No special tools or skills are needed and, provided the basic principles are followed, the design can easily be modified to suit alternative materials and components that are to hand.

PRINCIPLES OF OPERATION

The lunar, or synodic, month is twenty-nine days, twelve hours, forty-four minutes, and a few seconds long. For moon dials on domestic clocks, this is rounded down to twenty-nine and a half days, and the display has to be corrected slightly, once per year.

Commercial mechanisms vary, but a common practice is to paint two full moons on a disc which rotates, half hidden, behind the main dial plate. Semicircular screens projecting above the dial plate obscure the painted moons to create the effect of the changing lunar phases. Figs. 55, 56 and 57 illustrate the arrangement. Because there are two moons on the

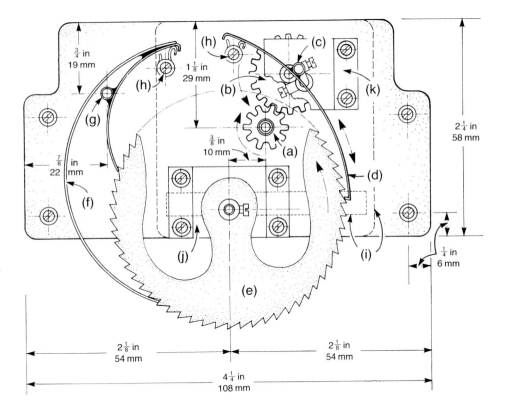

disc, it has to rotate once every fifty-nine days (i.e. $2 \times 29\frac{1}{2}$).

GENERAL DESCRIPTION OF THE MECHANISM

Figs. 47 and 48 depict the assembled unit. The hour shaft of a standard quartz movement is coupled by reduction gearing to a crankshaft

Fig 47 The moon dial mechanism viewed from the rear: (a) small gear wheel on movement hour shaft; (b) large gear wheel; (c) crank; (d) hooked arm; (e) ratchet wheel cut away to reveal its spindle bracket; (f) pawl with two vanes; (g) pawl pivot; (h) screws securing piano-wire springs; (i) profile of quartz movement behind base plate; (j) spindle bracket; (k) spindle bracket cut away to reveal gear.

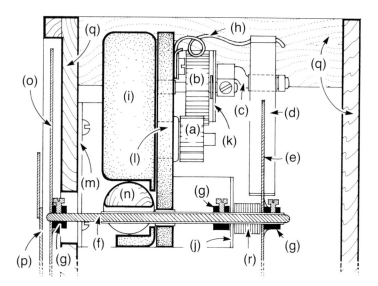

Fig 48 Section through moon dial mechanism: (a) small gear wheel; (b) large gear wheel; (c) crank; (d) hooked arm; (e) ratchet wheel; (f) moon disc spindle; (g) bushes; (h) piano-wire spring; (i) quartz movement; (j) moon disc spindle bracket; (k) large gear spindle bracket; (l) base plate; (m) mechanism fixing bracket; (n) wood dowel battery substitute; (o) moon disc; (p) dial plate; (q) inner case assembly; (r) packing washers.

which rotates once every twenty-four hours.

A metal strip with a hooked end is pivoted on the crankshaft and held against the rim of a fifty-nine toothed ratchet wheel by a light piano-wire spring. The rotating crank moves the metal strip backwards and forwards, and the hooked end of the strip pulls the ratchet wheel round, one tooth per day.

A second metal strip is pivoted and sprung so that its tip engages with the teeth. This strip acts as a pawl, to ensure that the wheel can rotate in only one direction. Without it, the wheel would just rock backwards and forwards under the action of the hooked arm.

The gearing enables the number of teeth on the ratchet to be reduced from 118 to fifty-nine, considerably easing the task of constructing the most critical part of the mechanism. Moreover, as this is a ratchet and not a gear wheel, great precision in the cutting of the teeth is not essential.

Crank offset is made adjustable so that the throw of the hooked arm can

be set to capture only one tooth at a time. Fig. 49 illustrates how this is done. By rotating the crank in its bush, it can be brought almost into alignment with the drive shaft, thereby creating the small amount of offset required.

A two-leaf pawl was found to be desirable in practice in order to overcome slight inconsistencies in the cutting of the teeth. The extra leaf ensures that the wheel is always locked while the hooked arm is reaching out to engage a tooth.

To keep the assembly as small as possible, the moon disc spindle is passed through the slot in the battery compartment of the quartz movement (the compartment is not accessible after the mechanism has been installed in the case), and the movement has to be externally powered.

The battery connectors in the movement will not accept lead/tin solder, so leads are connected by soldering wires to screws driven into the ends of a length of dowel, which is inserted in place of the dry cell. A

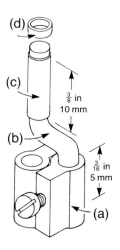

Fig 49 Enlarged view of moon dial crankshaft: (a) bushes from electrical terminal strip, sweated together; (b) cranked arm; (c) hooked arm pivot sleeve; (d) sleeve retaining ring or nut.

The moon-dial mechanism viewed from the pawl side. The fine piano wire springs, which engage the pawl and hooked arm are to the left of the ratchet wheel

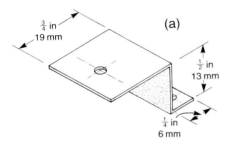

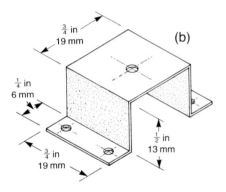

Fig 50 Spindle brackets: (a) large gear wheel and crankshaft bracket; (b) ratchet wheel and moon disc spindle bracket.

The mechanism viewed from the hooked arm side. The plastic reduction gears and the adjustable crankshaft are clearly visible

notch is cut in the dowel to clear the ratchet wheel spindle. This arrangement is also substituted for the battery in the clock movement, and both units are wired to a larger battery located in an easily accessible holder. Figs. 51 and 52 should make this clear.

The moon disc spindle slides inside the tubular spindle of the ratchet wheel. This optional refinement enables the spacing between the moon disc and the dial back plate to be adjusted without disturbing the mechanism.

Torque on the movement hour shaft is limited and the mechanism must move freely. Keep the springs which hold the pawl and the hooked arm against the ratchet as light as possible and avoid meshing the reduction gears too tightly.

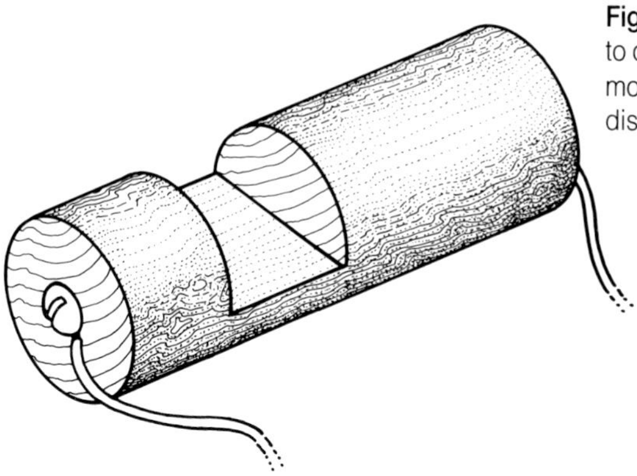

COMPONENTS AND MATERIALS

The Moon Dial Mechanism
- Brass strip, $\frac{1}{4} \times .016$ in (6×0.4 mm), for the pawl and hooked arm
- Brass tubing, $\frac{1}{8}$ in (3 mm) outside diameter, for the ratchet wheel and large gear wheel spindles, and the pivot sleeves for the pawl and hooked arm
- Brass rod, $\frac{3}{32}$ in (2.5 mm) diameter (a sliding fit in the above tube), for the crank and moon disc spindle
- Brass strip, $\frac{3}{4} \times .032$ in (19×0.8 mm) for the gear and ratchet wheel brackets (see also the time dial)
- Brass sheet, .016 in (0.4 mm) minimum thickness, for the ratchet wheel, moon disc, the two semicircular screens and the mechanism mounting brackets – all out of one piece, 6×6 in (152×152 mm)
- One off Junghans 738 quartz movement

- One off small plastic gear wheel, ten teeth, $\frac{1}{2}$ in (13 mm) diameter
- One off large plastic gear wheel, twenty teeth, $\frac{7}{8}$ in (22 mm) diameter
- Fine gauge (.015 in or 0.38 mm) piano wire, for the pawl and hooked arm springs
- Washers to fit $\frac{1}{8}$ in (3 mm) spindle
- One off, 5 amp electrical connector block (the type where separate terminals are set in a polythene strip)
- One off $1\frac{1}{2}$ in (38 mm) long bolt or length of studding, complete with two washers and four nuts, to act as a pivot for the pawl
- One off $\frac{3}{16}$ in (5 mm) thick Perspex (acrylic) or plywood sheet, $4\frac{1}{4} \times 2\frac{1}{4}$ in (108×57 mm) *finished* size for mechanism base plate
- Eight off $\frac{3}{16}$ in (5 mm) self-tapping screws, for assembling the mechanism
- Four off $\frac{1}{2} \times \frac{3}{32}$ in (13×2.5 mm) diameter bolts, complete with nuts and washers, to fix mechanism to brackets

The Time Dial
- One off square brass dial for use as back plate, $4\frac{5}{8} \times 4\frac{5}{8}$ in (118×118 mm); a square dial with a 4 in (104 mm) diameter time ring will usually be this size

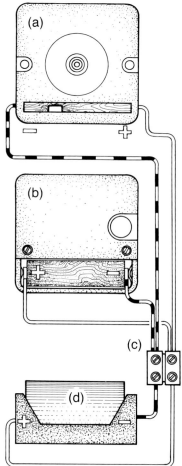

Fig 51 Wood dowel battery substitute, used to connect remote battery leads to movement. Note clearance notch for moon disc spindle.

Fig 52 Wiring diagram: (a) moon dial movement; (b) clock movement; (c) terminal block; (d) remote battery in holder.

- One off 4 in (104 mm) silver-effect chapter ring
- Four off spandrel cherubs $1\frac{9}{16}$ × $1\frac{1}{16}$ × $1\frac{1}{16}$ (40 × 27 × 27 mm)
- One pair of $1\frac{7}{8}$ in (47 mm) black serpentine hands
- One off quartz movement (a Junghans 738 Westminster chiming movement was installed by the author)
- Length of $\frac{3}{4}$ × .032 in (19 × 0.8 mm) brass strip for movement fixing brackets (see also strip for gear wheel brackets taken with moon dial mechanism)
- Twelve off $\frac{1}{4}$ in (6 mm) No. 4 dome-head brass screws for securing the dial back plate and the movement brackets (see also the screws for the battery substitutes)

The Dial Board and Inner Case Assembly
- Three off $\frac{3}{16}$ in (5 mm) thick plywood, 8 × $4\frac{3}{4}$ in (200 × 120 mm)
- One off $\frac{1}{2}$ in (13 mm) thick plywood, $4\frac{3}{4}$ × $2\frac{7}{8}$ in (120 × 75 mm), and two off hardwood struts, $\frac{5}{8}$ × $\frac{3}{8}$ in (16 × 9 mm), out of one 9 in (230 mm) length
- Four off $\frac{1}{2}$ in (13 mm) No. 6 countersunk brass screws, for securing the back panel
- Moulding pins, $\frac{3}{4}$ in (19 mm); brass ring pull and mesh for sound hole if Westminster movement fitted

The Electrical System
- 6 in (150 mm) of $\frac{1}{2}$ in (13 mm) diameter dowel for the two battery substitutes
- Four off $\frac{1}{4}$ in (6 mm) No. 4 dome-head brass screws to act as contacts and lead anchorages on the battery substitutes

- One off battery holder for a type C dry cell (HP11, AM2, etc.), complete with fixing screws
- One off two-way terminal strip (cut from length itemized above), complete with fixing screws
- Red and black plastic insulated tinned copper wire

Sundries
- Flux cored solder and soldering iron. The glues, stains, paints, varnishes and other finishing materials have already been listed in Chapters One and Four.

Notes on the Above Items
Brass rod, tube, strip angle and sheet are sold in 12 in (305 mm) lengths, and a wide range of interlocking sizes, in model shops throughout the United Kingdom, Australia, Canada and North America. Suitable plastic gear wheels can also be obtained from most model shops or from the suppliers who advertise in magazines devoted to model making.

A 12 in (305 mm) length of each of the specified rods, tubes and strips will be more than sufficient to complete the dial.

CONSTRUCTING THE MECHANISM AND MOON DISC

The Mechanism
① Cut out the base plate. Drill the hole for the movement only at this stage. Fix the movement in position.

② Cut out, drill and form the two spindle brackets (see Fig. 50).

③ Drill and then gently ream out the spindle hole in the ten-tooth gear wheel until it is a firm push-fit on the

hour shaft of the movement. Fit the gear in position.

④ Fit the spindle in the twenty-tooth gear wheel, mount it in its bracket and hold it in position, lightly meshed, with the ten-tooth wheel. Mark the position of the bracket fixing holes on the base plate.

⑤ Mark the position of the hole for the ratchet wheel spindle. It must be on the centre line of the plate and aligned with the slot in the battery compartment of the movement.

⑥ Remove the movement from the base plate. Mark out the remaining holes and complete the drilling work. Size the holes to suit the self-tapping fixing screws and the brass tubing used as spindles.

⑦ Mount the movement, gears and ratchet wheel spindle bracket on the base plate. Measure the distance between the ratchet wheel spindle and the crankshaft spindle. This distance, less the crankshaft offset and a little clearance, is the maximum size of the ratchet wheel. With the final version of the mechanism, $\frac{3}{8}$ in (9 mm) was deducted from $1\frac{5}{8}$ in (41 mm) to give a ratchet wheel outer radius of $1\frac{1}{4}$ in (32 mm).

⑧ Using compasses with a steel point in place of the pencil lead, mark out the wheel on sheet brass. Scribe another circle $\frac{1}{16}$ in (1.5 mm) in from the circumference to indicate the depth of the teeth. This is not too critical, but avoid making the teeth deeper, and therefore steeper, than necessary.

⑨ Cut out the disc with tin snips or strong scissors and flatten any twist in the vice.

⑩ Lay the disc on the template in Fig. 53, carefully aligning the centres, and use a sharp metal stylus to scribe the fifty-nine teeth points. Because of the odd number of teeth, they must be marked out individually; it is not possible to scribe across the centre and set out two teeth with one pass. The small markers on the outer rim of the template give 118 divisions for the experimentally minded, who may wish to design other mechanisms.

⑪ Cut the teeth with scissors or tin snips, using the inner circle as a depth guide (see Fig. 47). Keep the size and depth of the teeth as constant as possible, and gently flatten the wheel in the vice on completion.

⑫ Cut the lengths of strip, rod, tube and piano wire which make up the remainder of the mechanism. Remove three electrical terminals from their polythene housing and cut them in half to yield six spindle bushes with fixing screws (five are required).

⑬ Tin and sweat together two of the bushes to form the crank offset adjuster, as illustrated in Fig. 49. Form the crank from brass rod and mount the assembly on the spindle of the large gear wheel.

⑭ Tin and sweat together the hooked arm and its pivot tube. Mount the arm on the crank and check that it is parallel to the base plate and free-moving.

⑮ Tin and sweat together the ends of the long and short pawl arms. Tin and sweat the short pawl arm to its pivot tube.

⑯ Push the 1½ in (38 mm) long bolt through the base plate and secure it

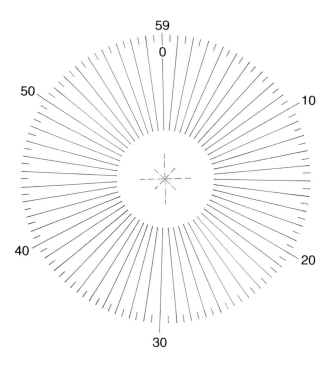

Fig 53 Protractor for setting out the fifty-nine-tooth ratchet wheel.

with a nut, fitting washers on either side of the plate. Slide the pawl pivot tube on to this bolt and fit lock nuts to hold it in place. Check that the pawl moves freely, is parallel to the plate and the same height above the plate as the hooked arm.

⑰ Tin a spindle bush and the centre of the ratchet wheel and sweat them together. Note that the bush is fixed on the outside of the wheel.

⑱ Fix the ratchet wheel on its tubular spindle and slide it into position. Place washers on the spindle to bring the wheel into alignment with the pawl and hooked arm. Check that the wheel is free-running and flat enough to stay in alignment. Remember to slide the retaining bush on to the spindle; this is located beneath the bracket.

A smaller-diameter brass disc was bolted to the ratchet wheel in order to

stiffen it. This refinement is not absolutely necesssary, but constructors may wish to duplicate it.

⑲ Bend the pawl arms to shape. Make the sharp, acute-angle bend which forms the hook at the tip of the hooked arm. Bend the arms at the spring ends to prevent the springs sliding off, all as shown in Fig. 47.

⑳ Form the piano-wire springs, coiling them a couple of times at the base-plate end. Fix the springs to the base plate by clamping them beneath washers held down by self-tapping screws.

㉑ Assemble the mechanisms minus the small gear wheel. Rotate the large gear wheel by hand to operate the crank. The hooked arm should move backwards and forwards, pulling the ratchet wheel around, while the pawl arms click as they drop between the teeth. Adjust the pawl arms so they both engage with the wheel. Adjust the crank offset so the hooked arm travels slightly more than one tooth. Adjust the springs so that the pawl and hooked arm engage with the wheel positively but with a minimum of pressure.

㉒ Remove the ratchet wheel and fit the small gear wheel in position on the hour shaft of the movement. Replace the ratchet wheel.

㉓ Construct the wooden battery substitute and cut a notch in it to clear the ratchet wheel spindle. Insert it in the movement and connect the leads to a separate battery in a holder. Observe battery polarity or the clock will not run.

㉔ Mark the ratchet wheel with a tiny spot of paint, record the date and time, and leave the assembly on test. This trial run will reveal any under- or over-shooting of the hooked arm and any failure of the pawls to prevent clockwise rotation.

The Moon Disc
① Cut out the brass moon disc, tin the centre and tin a spindle bush. Sweat bush and disc together. Mount the disc on the inner spindle rod and very gently bend it flat and true: if there is excessive buckling the disc will bind against the dial board and dial back plate.

② Cut the two semicircles of brass which screen the moon disc. Polish disc and semicircles to a brilliant shine and coat them with clear cellulose (coat the semicircles on both sides).

③ Mix cobalt and ultramarine blue artist's acrylic colour and thin with a

The moon dial

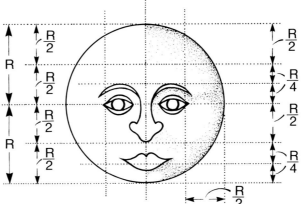

Fig 54 Moon face proportions.

little water, as necessary. Apply two or three even coats to disc and screens to ensure an opaque finish.

Artists' acrylic colour does not adhere well to bare metal and the clear cellulose is necessary as a primer. Nor does the colour flow well on non-absorbent surfaces. Flow improver is sold by the colour manufacturers and its use would no doubt ensure a smoother finish than

was achieved by the author. Leave the painted parts to harden overnight.

④ Apply two coats of artists' white acrylic colour to self-adhesive paper labels, then draw in pencil the two $1\frac{1}{8}$ in (29 mm) diameter moons. A guide to setting out the features is given in Fig. 54. The white acrylic colour must be applied to prevent the paper moons being discoloured by the sealing process mentioned in (5), below. Using the artist's No. 2 brush, line in the features with a mixture of white and red iron oxide acrylic colour.

Cut out the moons and stick them to the moon disc, all as illustrated in Figs. 55 and 56.

⑤ Using a needle or pointed scriber, scratch through the blue colour on the disc and screens to form stars by exposing the brass. Draw the scriber

from the tip to the centre of the star for the best results. Vary the size of the stars and scatter them in a random fashion.

When screens and disc are satisfactory, seal them with a single coat of clear, matt, polyurethane varnish.

The Dial Board and Inner Case Assembly

Moon dials and time dial are mounted on a built-up plywood dial board. This is linked by a plywood base and

top struts to the back panel of the clock case. By this means, the whole assembly can be pulled, like a drawer, from the outer case, giving easy access to the mechanism, time movement and battery.

The arrangement is illustrated in Figs. 48, 57 and 72, and in the photograph on page 51. Construction should proceed as follows.

① Cut three pieces of $\frac{3}{16}$ in (5 mm) thick plywood, each $8 \times 4\frac{3}{4}$ in (200 ×

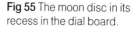

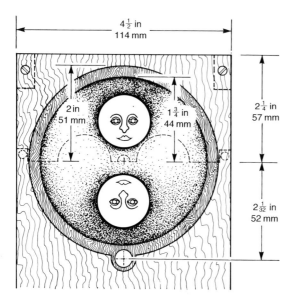

Fig 55 The moon disc in its recess in the dial board.

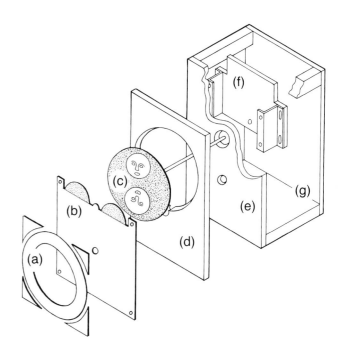

Fig 56 Setting-out details for the moon disc and the semicircular screens.

Fig 57 View of dials and inner case assembly: (a) chapter ring and spandrels; (b) dial back plate; (c) moon disc; (d) dial board front sheet; (e) dial board back sheet (cut away); (f) moon dial mechanism base plate; (g) inner case assembly.

120 mm). Clamp them together in the vice and plane them square, true and down to a finished size of $7\frac{3}{4} \times 4\frac{1}{2}$ in (196 × 114 mm). Two of these are required for the built-up dial board, the other for the back of the case.

② Clamp the two pieces of the dial board together and drill the hole for the movement spindle through both.

③ Part the pieces and cut the 4 in (102 mm) diameter hole which forms the recess for the moon disc in the outer board. Drill a $\frac{1}{2}$ in (13 mm) diameter hole for the moon disc spindle in the inner board (to give clearance for the spindle bush and screw). Glue the two pieces together with PVA adhesive.

④ Cut the base for the inner case assembly from $\frac{1}{2}$ in (13 mm) plywood and plane it square, true and to a finished size of $4\frac{1}{4} \times 2\frac{5}{8}$ in (114 × 67 mm).

⑤ Cut the two top struts from $\frac{5}{8} \times \frac{3}{8}$ in (16 × 9 mm) mahogany and disc-sand the ends square, true and to a finished length of $2\frac{5}{8}$ in (67 mm).

⑥ Glue and pin the base and struts to the dial board.

⑦ The back panel, which is also the back of the case, is secured to the base and struts by means of four $\frac{1}{2}$ in (13 mm) No. 6 brass screws. Drill and countersink the holes for these screws and drill thread holes. If a Westminster chiming movement is to be fitted, form a 3 in (75 mm) diameter sound hole in the back panel.

⑧ Glasspaper smooth, stain and button polish the entire inner case assembly.

THE MOON AND TIME DIALS

The Moon Dial

① Construct the mounting brackets for the moon dial mechanism, as shown in Fig. 58. Note the slotted holes, which permit vertical adjustment of the mechanism. Fix the brackets to the rear of the dial board with $\frac{1}{4}$ in (6 mm) No. 4 screws. With the battery substitute inserted in the moon dial movement, fix the mechanism to the brackets.

② Fix the moon disc to its spindle rod and slide it, telescope fashion, into the tubular spindle of the ratchet wheel. Lock it in position with the ratchet wheel screw (this screw will squeeze the outer tube and secure disc and wheel).

The Time Dial

① Trim the width of the brass dial back plate to fit the dial board; this is best done before the inner case is assembled. Cut the top of the plate to the profile given in Fig. 56 (note the tabs for fixing the semicircular screens). Drill fixing holes, one at each corner.

② Cut, bend and drill the time movement rear-fixing brackets (see previous chapter for details). Fix the time movement in position.

③ Fix the chapter ring, spandrels and semicircular blue-painted screens to the brass back plate. Screens and plate have previously been coated with clear cellulose so they can be stuck together with balsa cement.

④ Fix the dial assembly to the dial board with four $\frac{1}{4}$ in (6 mm) No. 4 dome-headed brass screws. Fix the hands to the movement.

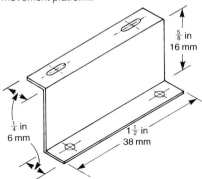

Fig 58 Mechanism mounting brackets: slotted holes permit vertical adjustment of movement platform.

WIRING UP THE MOVEMENTS AND COMPLETING THE ASSEMBLY

① Fix the battery holder and a two-way terminal block (cut from the strip used for the spindle bushes) to the bottom of the inner case.

② Insert the wood dowel battery substitute in the time movement and connect both movements to the battery holder via the terminal block, all as illustrated in Fig. 52. Observe polarity.

③ Fix a protective mesh over any sound hole in the back panel and secure the panel in position by means of four $\frac{1}{2}$ in (13 mm) No. 6 screws. Fix a ring pull to the rear panel; this makes it easier to withdraw the entire assembly from the outer case.

Set the moon dial at the time of the full or new moon by gently rotating the ratchet wheel in an anticlockwise direction.

If the outer case is made before the inner dial assembly, the dimensions of the dial board, base, struts and case back may need adjusting slightly to suit it.

PART TWO

Sharp Gothic, pillar and scroll and
round-cased Grecian clocks

Introductory Notes

DRAWINGS AND DIMENSIONS

Dimensions are given in inches and millimetres on the drawings, and complicated decorative features and mouldings are reproduced full-size. Gaps around dial boards and false and true doors have been exaggerated to make the construction clear. These gaps should, of course, be no wider than is necessary for free movement after the finishes have been applied. Side views are included only where they are necessary for an understanding of the construction or decoration of a case. In most instances, the cross-section conveys all of the information required.

When the depth or width of a case is quoted, this is, unless indicated to the contrary, the external dimension of the basic box, excluding the projection of base or top mouldings. Capital letters on the drawings relate to the tables of alternative dimensions; lower-case letters refer to the adjoining caption.

Metric equivalents are given on the drawings, in the text and in the tables. The equivalents have been rounded up or down, as appropriate, to suit the particular dimension or component. Sometimes the closest metric equivalents are quoted for certain parts, even though the dimensions do not precisely coincide. Examples of this are 4 in (104 mm) diameter chapter rings and 4 in (100 mm) diameter bezels.

LARGER CASES

Typical dimensions of the original antiques are given to guide anyone interested in full-size replicas, and the tables of alternative dimensions cover a range of bezel, dial and chapter ring diameters. Before embarking on a larger version of a case, it is a good idea to make a cardboard cutout, or even a rough cardboard box, the same size as the proposed clock, and view it in the chosen location. Cutting lists will, of course, need to be revised if larger versions of the clocks are constructed.

Mouldings can be scaled up by carefully drawing the profile within the framework of the new dimensions; few are sufficiently complicated to warrant the use of the squared-grid technique.

CUTTING LISTS

Many of the parts included in the lists are small and would normally be cut from scrap material. The lists have, however, been made as comprehensive as possible in order to convey more clearly the method of construction.

Unless otherwise stated, the sizes are sawn sizes and include a planing or turning allowance of at least $\frac{1}{8}$ in (3 mm) for each sawn face. *Finished* sizes are given for the cross-sections of mouldings, door-frame members and slender strips, but the stated lengths allow for waste in cutting and mitring. Grain direction is normally parallel to the longest dimension.

Veneer areas include sufficient material for trimming about $\frac{1}{2}$ in (13 mm) around each laid piece, but veneer is not included for case backs and bottoms. Turning blanks for bun feet have been made long enough to accommodate twice the required number, so that well-matched sets can be selected.

Many of the mouldings were built up from separate strips, as this tends to produce the best results, especially when the profile is complicated. Constructors wishing to attempt one-piece mouldings with the scratch stock will need to combine items in the cutting lists.

Adhesives and finishing materials, including the furniture-protecting pads of green baize or felt, are common to all of the clocks. These items are considered in detail in earlier chapters and are not repeated in the lists of components. Dimensions are not given for the door glass, as this needs to be cut to fit the rebates of the doors, as constructed.

CHAPTER SEVEN

A Renaissance Domed Clock

HISTORY AND DERIVATION

The flowering of culture and learning known as the Renaissance began in Italy during the fourteenth century and, over the next 300 years, spread throughout Europe. Artists and craftsmen rejected the Gothic style and turned to the ancient world of the Greeks and Romans for their inspiration, rediscovering classical architectural forms and orders.

The decorative arts followed the prevailing fashion. By the sixteenth century, a clock-case style had evolved and become popular in most European countries. Made of gilded copper or brass, these cases were square or hexagonal in plan and decorated with base mouldings, dados, friezes, cornices and domes. Often adorned with turned finials and engravings of scenes from Greek and Roman mythology, they have come to be known as Renaissance clocks.

The antique originals ranged in height from a diminutive 3 in (75 mm) to about 12 in (300 mm), but 8 in (200 mm) tall versions seem to have been the most popular. A mahogany case in this style, constructed during the Regency period by Benjamin Louis Vulliamy, clockmaker to King George IV of England, measures $31\frac{1}{4}$ in (795 mm) to the crown of the dome. Displayed in London at the British Museum, it has a circular white dial and five pineapple finials. Bezel diameter is $8\frac{1}{4}$ in (210 mm) and the dome finial is $5\frac{1}{2}$ in (140 mm) tall.

CHAPTER NINE

A Basket Top Bracket Clock

HISTORY AND DERIVATION

The basket top clock was fashionable between about 1680 and 1715. It was the first widely popular style to emerge in England after the introduction of the pendulum. Perhaps the increased demand for smaller, spring-driven clocks had brought about a specialization in the cabinet-making trade and this, in turn, had resulted in some standardization of case design.

Early versions had plain wooden baskets. On later models, the baskets were either decorated with, or formed entirely from, pierced and gilded brass. The similarity between this pierced metalwork and a basket gave the clock its name. Ornate brass urns were sometimes added to the top of the case, one at each corner, together with additional pierced decoration to the stiles and rails of the doors.

These cases were often of ebony veneer on oak or of ebonized pearwood. Although the basic form is always clearly identifiable, individual clockmakers displayed preferences in matters of detail, and feet, mouldings and decorations vary.

The antique originals ranged in size from about 12 in (300 mm) to 18 in (450 mm) high, excluding the handle, but 12 in (300 mm) tall clocks with bun feet and 6 in (150 mm) chapter rings seem to have been the most popular. Miniature versions, about 8 in tall (200 mm), were produced by London makers early in the eighteenth century, presumably for use as travelling clocks, but surviving examples are extremely rare.

Fig 66 Front view of basket top case.

GENERAL DETAILS OF THE DESIGN

The clock is shown in the photograph opposite and in Figs. 66, 67 and 68.

The ornate handle is a simplified version of a type favoured by some of the original makers and the winged cherubs are a very typical feature.

If the clock is to be embellished with urns or pineapple decorations, the top moulding should be made flush with the top of the case to provide a flat area to accommodate the finials, which should be about $1\frac{3}{8}$ in (35 mm) tall.

Turned bun feet were fitted to this case. Turned wooden feet were not unknown, but brass buns seem to have been more common. Basket and base moulding have been made fairly tall, and the height of the door emphasized slightly, in order to prevent the case appearing squat.

Choice of Wood

The case was constructed from Brazilian mahogany. This wood is easily worked to a good finish, takes stain well and matching machine-cut scotia is available from most timber merchants. It is, however, not an authentic choice for the basket top clock (mahogany did not become popular until about 1760): walnut, oak veneered with ebony or ebonized pearwood are the traditional materials for this case.

MATERIALS AND COMPONENTS

Cutting List

The case shell was made from plywood and veneered. Constructors who prefer to use solid hardwood can substitute this for the plywood and delete the veneer.

The following out of $\frac{1}{2}$ in (13 mm) plywood:
- Case sides, two off, $8\frac{1}{4} \times 3\frac{1}{2}$ in (210 × 90 mm)
- Top and bottom, two off, $7\frac{1}{8} \times 3\frac{1}{2}$ in (180 × 90 mm)
- Rear door, one off, $8\frac{1}{4} \times 6\frac{1}{8}$ in (210 × 155 mm)

The following out of $\frac{3}{8}$ in (9 mm) plywood:
- Dial board, one off, $8\frac{1}{4} \times 6\frac{1}{8}$ in (210 × 155 mm)

Strips, in the following, *finished* sizes:
- Basket top plate, out of $4 \times 1\frac{1}{8} \times \frac{1}{8}$ in (102 × 29 × 3 mm)
- Basket sides, out of $30 \times 1 \times 1\frac{1}{8}$ in (760 × 25 × 29 mm)
- Basket base mouldings, out of $30 \times 1\frac{3}{16} \times \frac{3}{8}$ in (760 × 30 × 9 mm)

Fig 67 Transverse section through basket top case, looking towards glazed door.

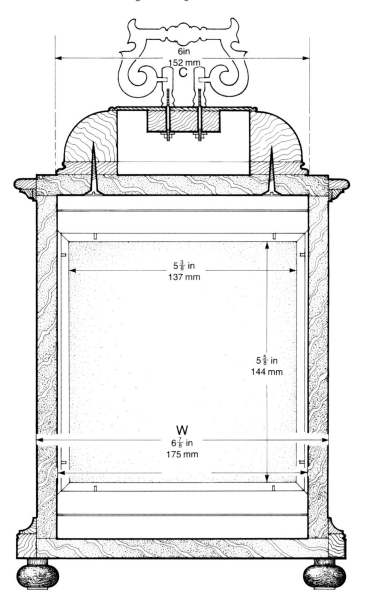

The basket top bracket clock

CHAPTER TEN

Bell Top Clocks

HISTORY AND DERIVATION

The inverted bell top case superseded the basket top around 1715 and its introduction coincided with the development of the break-arch dial. Clockmakers used this additional, semicircular dial area for strike-silent settings, plates bearing their names, *tempus fugit* mottoes, and day of the month and moon dials.

The true bell top clock followed around 1760, and both types remained fashionable throughout the eighteenth century. Indeed, from the eighteenth century on, styles agglomerate rather than evolve, and copies of early clocks are still being produced.

Around 1750, circular white dials with brass bezels began to be fitted to inverted bell top cases. Clocks modified in this way were simpler and less expensive to construct, and the front panel was square rather than rectangular to suit the circular dial. The reduction in height made the clocks less elegant, and this rather radical innovation does not seem to have been very popular. Size tended to increase as the century progressed. Some of the larger examples were fitted with side handles and a pineapple finial was substituted for the handle at the top.

The height of the original cases, excluding the handle, ranged from approximately 12 in (300 mm) to 26 in (660 mm), with around 18 in (450 mm) being a popular size.

The inverted bell top clock

Fig 69 Front view of inverted bell top clock.

Fig 70 Front view of bell top clock.

GENERAL DETAILS OF THE DESIGN

The clocks are shown in the photographs on pages 75 and 78, and in Figs. 69, 70, 71, 72 and 73. The cases are identical, apart from the bell-top mouldings. Alternative dials are detailed, and a white dial with cathedral hands would also be appropriate (white dials were introduced around 1750). Guidance on making decorated card dials for these clocks is given in Chapter Five.

The plain handle and block feet were very typical and ought not to be changed. Pineapple finials were often fitted at the top corners of these cases. If this decoration is to be applied, the corners of the bell top base mouldings will have to be scribed around the finials as there is only a narrow margin of flat top on this design. Finials about 1 in (25 mm) high would be suitable for the case as detailed.

Choice of Wood

Brazilian mahogany was used for these cases. Mahogany became fashionable after about 1760 and the choice is, therefore, authentic as well as pleasing to the eye. Cases of this kind were often ebonized and this treatment would also be appropriate.

MATERIALS AND COMPONENTS

Cutting List

The case shells were made from plywood and veneered. The cutting list is based on this and on a clock with a time dial only. If a moon dial is to be installed, a cutting and components list for the entire dial and inner case assembly is given in Chapter Six.

The following out of $\frac{1}{2}$ in (13 mm) plywood:
- Case sides, two off, $8 \times 3\frac{3}{4}$ in (203×95 mm)
- Top and bottom, two off, $5\frac{3}{4} \times 3\frac{3}{4}$ in (146×95 mm)
- Rear door, one off, $8 \times 4\frac{3}{4}$ in (203×120 mm)

The following out of $\frac{3}{8}$ in (9 mm) plywood:
- Dial board, one off, $8 \times 4\frac{3}{4}$ in (203×120 mm)

Strips, in the following, *finished* sizes:
Inverted bell top crown moulding:
- Top plate, one off, $2\frac{3}{4} \times \frac{3}{4} \times \frac{7}{16}$ ($70 \times 19 \times 11$ mm)
- Top bead, out of $9 \times \frac{1}{8} \times \frac{1}{8}$ in ($230 \times 3 \times 3$ mm)
- Bell sides built up from $24 \times 1\frac{1}{4} \times 1\frac{1}{8}$ in ($610 \times 32 \times 29$ mm) and $24 \times \frac{1}{8} \times \frac{1}{8}$ in ($610 \times 3 \times 3$ mm), and scotia, $15 \times \frac{1}{2} \times \frac{1}{2}$ in ($380 \times 13 \times 13$ mm)

True bell top crown moulding:
- Top plate, one off, $2\frac{1}{2} \times \frac{3}{4} \times \frac{1}{8}$ in ($64 \times 19 \times 3$ mm)
- Bell sides built up from $18 \times \frac{3}{4} \times \frac{1}{2}$ in ($460 \times 19 \times 13$ mm), $18 \times \frac{11}{16} \times \frac{3}{32}$ in ($460 \times 18 \times 2$ mm), $18 \times \frac{5}{8} \times \frac{7}{16}$ in ($460 \times 16 \times 11$ mm), $24 \times \frac{3}{8} \times \frac{7}{8}$ in ($610 \times 9 \times 22$ mm and $24 \times \frac{1}{8} \times \frac{1}{8}$ in ($610 \times 3 \times 3$ mm), and scotia, $24 \times \frac{7}{8} \times \frac{7}{8}$ in ($610 \times 22 \times 22$ mm)

Case parts common to both versions of the design:
- Top moulding, built up from $48 \times \frac{3}{8} \times \frac{9}{32}$ in ($1,220 \times 9 \times 7$ mm) and $24 \times \frac{7}{16} \times \frac{3}{16}$ in ($610 \times 11 \times 5$ mm)

Fig 71 Transverse section through inverted bell top and bell top cases, looking towards glazed false door. Crown moulding omitted and case side cut away to expose door stile.

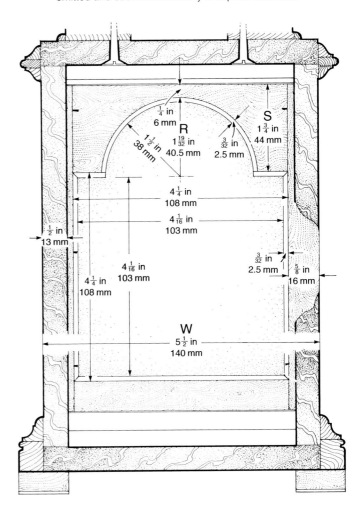

The bell top clock

- Door top rail, one off, $4\frac{1}{2} \times 1\frac{3}{4} \times \frac{1}{4}$ in (114 × 44 × 6 mm)
- Door stiles and bottom rail, $24 \times \frac{3}{8} \times \frac{5}{8}$ in (610 × 9 × 16 mm)
- Glazing bead, $18 \times \frac{5}{16} \times \frac{3}{32}$ in (460 × 8 × 2 mm)
- Dial board spacers and rear door stop lath, out of $18 \times \frac{1}{4} \times \frac{1}{4}$ in (460 × 6 × 6 mm)
- Base mouldings, built up from $24 \times \frac{7}{16} \times \frac{1}{2}$ in (610 × 11 × 13 mm) and $24 \times \frac{1}{2} \times \frac{5}{8}$ in (610 × 13 × 15 mm)
- Top packing piece, $6 \times \frac{3}{8} \times \frac{29}{32}$ in (150 × 9 × 23 mm)
- Bottom packing piece, $6 \times \frac{3}{8} \times 1\frac{7}{32}$ in (150 × 9 × 31 mm)
- Feet, four off, out of $9 \times 1 \times \frac{3}{8}$ in (230 × 25 × 9 mm)
- Handle mounting block out of scrap

Veneer

A short leaf of veneer, 36 × 6 in (920 × 152 mm) will provide sufficient material. If the bell top is to be veneered, an 8 in (200 mm) wide leaf is required.

OTHER MATERIALS AND COMPONENTS

- Quartz movement
- Silver-effect chapter ring, 4 in (104 mm) diameter
- Pair of black serpentine hands, $1\frac{7}{8}$ in (47 mm)
- Square brass dials, two off (one for back plate and one to provide brass sheet for arch dial), 4 in nominal size, $4\frac{5}{8} \times 4\frac{5}{8}$ in (118 × 118 mm) actual
- Brass strip for movement fixing brackets, $3 \times \frac{3}{4} \times$ .032 in (76 × 19 × 0.8 mm)
- Eight $\frac{1}{4}$ in (6 mm) No. 4 screws for securing the movement and the dial back plate
- Four $\frac{1}{2}$ in (13 mm) No. 6 screws for retaining the dial board
- Scrolled spandrel decorations, four off, $1\frac{3}{4} \times 1\frac{5}{16} \times 1\frac{5}{16}$ in (45 × 33 × 33 mm)
- Handle, $2\frac{1}{8} \times 1\frac{3}{8}$ in high (54 × 35 mm)
- Large cherub for arch dial, one off, $3\frac{1}{8} \times 2\frac{1}{8} \times 2\frac{1}{8}$ in (80 × 55 × 55 mm)
- Two pairs of $\frac{3}{4}$ in (19 mm) brass hinges, complete with screws for one pair
- Brass hook-and-eye fastener for rear door, $\frac{3}{4}$ in (19 mm)
- Glass and glazing sprigs

CONSTRUCTION

Detailed guidance is given in Chapter Three. If a moon dial is to be fitted, full constructional details are given in

Chapter Six. The door glass passes behind the top rail, thereby avoiding the need to cut it to a stepped and curved shape. Check before assembly that there is just sufficient room to insert glazing sprigs into the stiles and, if necessary, reduce the thickness of the top rail slightly. This should be required only if $\frac{5}{64}$ in (2 mm) glass is fitted.

These clocks usually had side panels of pierced brasswork so that the sound of chimes could be more easily heard. Observations made in earlier chapters regarding framed construction and side panels apply to larger versions of this timepiece also.

Case dimensions to suit a range of chapter-ring diameters are given in the table.

CLOCK DIMENSION			CHAPTER-RING DIAMETER			
			4 in 104 mm	5 in 127 mm	6 in 152 mm	7 in 178 mm
H	HEIGHT OF CASE	in	$8\frac{3}{4}$	$10\frac{11}{16}$	$12\frac{7}{8}$	15
		mm	222	271	327	380
D	DEPTH OF CASE	in	$3\frac{7}{8}$	$4\frac{5}{8}$	$5\frac{3}{8}$	$6\frac{3}{8}$
		mm	99	117	137	162
W	WIDTH OF CASE	in	$5\frac{1}{2}$	$6\frac{3}{4}$	$8\frac{1}{8}$	$9\frac{1}{2}$
		mm	140	171	206	240
A	BELL HEIGHT	in	$2\frac{1}{16}$	$2\frac{1}{2}$	3	$3\frac{1}{2}$
		mm	52	63	76	89
B	BELL DEPTH	in	$3\frac{1}{4}$	$3\frac{7}{8}$	$4\frac{3}{8}$	$5\frac{1}{4}$
		mm	83	98	111	134
C	BELL WIDTH	in	$4\frac{7}{8}$	6	$7\frac{1}{8}$	$8\frac{3}{8}$
		mm	124	152	181	212
E	TOP MOULDING	in	$\frac{7}{16} \times \frac{3}{4}$	$\frac{1}{2} \times \frac{7}{8}$	$\frac{5}{8} \times 1\frac{1}{8}$	$\frac{3}{4} \times 1\frac{1}{4}$
		mm	11 × 19	13 × 23	16 × 28	19 × 32
F	BASE MOULDING	in	$\frac{1}{2} \times 1\frac{1}{8}$	$\frac{5}{8} \times 1\frac{3}{8}$	$\frac{3}{4} \times 1\frac{5}{8}$	$\frac{7}{8} \times 1\frac{7}{8}$
		mm	13 × 28	16 × 35	19 × 42	22 × 48
G	FEET	in	$1 \times 1 \times \frac{3}{8}$	$1\frac{1}{4} \times 1\frac{1}{4} \times \frac{7}{16}$	$1\frac{1}{2} \times 1\frac{1}{2} \times \frac{1}{2}$	$1\frac{3}{4} \times 1\frac{3}{4} \times \frac{5}{8}$
		mm	25 × 25 × 9	32 × 32 × 11	37 × 37 × 13	43 × 43 × 16
J	DOOR STILES & BOTTOM RAIL	in	$\frac{3}{8} \times \frac{5}{8}$	$\frac{1}{2} \times \frac{3}{4}$	$\frac{1}{2} \times \frac{7}{8}$	$\frac{5}{8} \times 1\frac{1}{16}$
		mm	9 × 16	13 × 19	13 × 23	16 × 27
K	GLAZING BEAD	in	$\frac{5}{16} \times \frac{3}{32}$	$\frac{3}{8} \times \frac{1}{8}$	$\frac{3}{8} \times \frac{1}{8}$	$\frac{1}{2} \times \frac{5}{32}$
		mm	8 × 2.5	9 × 3	9 × 3	13 × 4
R	ARCH RADIUS	in	$1\frac{19}{32}$	$1\frac{15}{16}$	$2\frac{5}{16}$	$2\frac{3}{4}$
		mm	40.5	49	59	69
S	DOOR TOP RAIL	in	$1\frac{3}{4} \times \frac{1}{4}$	$2\frac{3}{16} \times \frac{5}{16}$	$2\frac{5}{8} \times \frac{5}{16}$	$3\frac{1}{16} \times \frac{13}{32}$
		mm	44 × 6	56 × 8	66 × 8	77 × 10

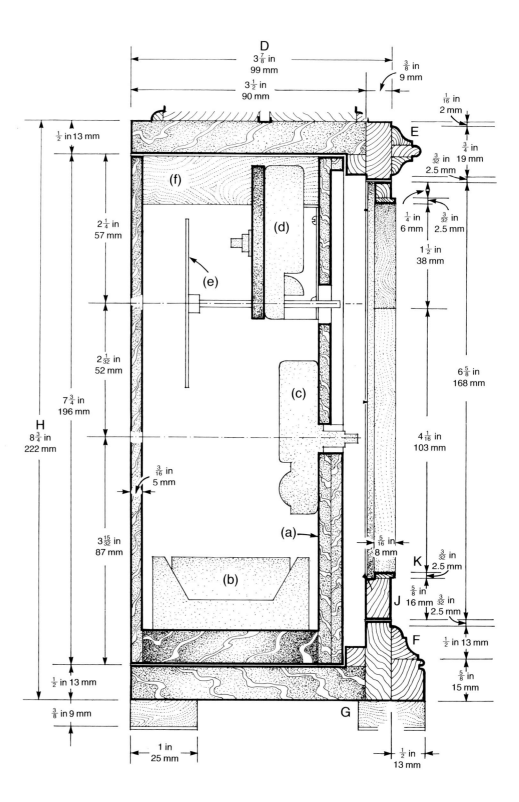

Fig 72 Section through inverted bell top and bell top cases (version with moon dial and associated inner case assembly). Crown moulding, moon disc, moon dial mechanism, time dial and hands omitted: (a) built-up dial board; (b) battery holder; (c) time movement; (d) moon dial movement; (e) ratchet wheel; (f) top strut.

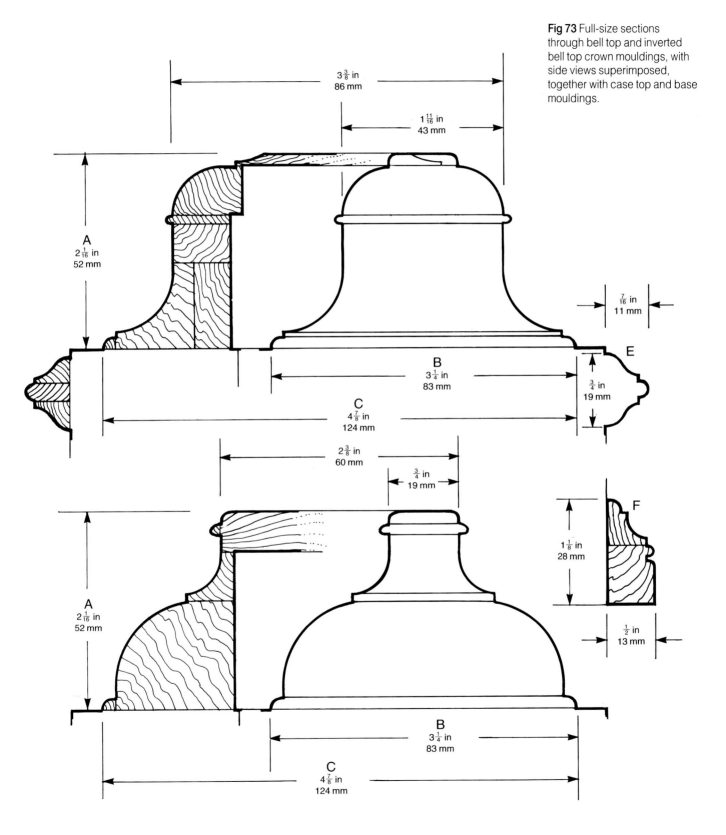

Fig 73 Full-size sections through bell top and inverted bell top crown mouldings, with side views superimposed, together with case top and base mouldings.

$3\frac{3}{8}$ in
86 mm

$1\frac{11}{16}$ in
43 mm

A
$2\frac{1}{16}$ in
52 mm

$\frac{7}{16}$ in
11 mm

E

B
$3\frac{1}{4}$ in
83 mm

$\frac{3}{4}$ in
19 mm

C
$4\frac{7}{8}$ in
124 mm

$2\frac{3}{8}$ in
60 mm

$\frac{3}{4}$ in
19 mm

F

$1\frac{1}{8}$ in
28 mm

A
$2\frac{1}{16}$ in
52 mm

$\frac{1}{2}$ in
13 mm

B
$3\frac{1}{4}$ in
83 mm

C
$4\frac{7}{8}$ in
124 mm

CHAPTER ELEVEN

A Balloon Clock

HISTORY AND DERIVATION

Towards the end of the reign of Louis XV the French, who were prolific case designers, produced what eventually became known as the balloon clock.

Clocks of this type pre-dated by about twenty years the first manned balloon flight by the Montgolfier brothers in 1783. Whether or not their experiments with rigid hot-air balloons inspired the design is a matter for conjecture, but the clock was known in France as a 'pendule montgolfier' and the ballooning adventures of the two brothers no doubt helped to make it popular. The style became fashionable in England, where in the main the case was less ornate and the shape more balloon-like in outline. However, painted decoration, often comprising birds, drapery and garlands of flowers, was occasionally applied to satinwood versions, particularly by London makers.

Cases of this type produced during the eighteenth and nineteenth centuries ranged in height from about 10 in (250 mm) to 24 in (600 mm), excluding any finial. Smaller examples subsequently became popular, with the neck sometimes being narrowed down to as little as half the radius of the top in order to produce a more dramatic profile.

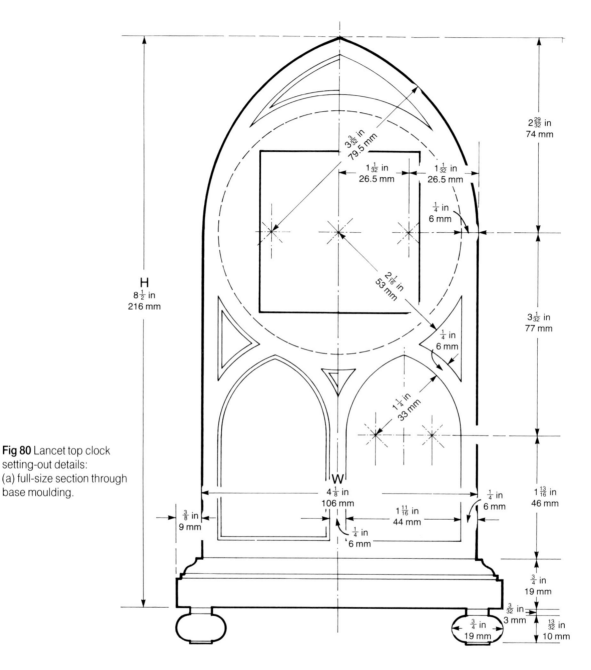

Fig 80 Lancet top clock setting-out details: (a) full-size section through base moulding.

such as those ruled on to the arch top clock shown in the photograph on page 95, will be more appropriate if wood with a very pronounced grain pattern is used.

The caddy feet and ring handles applied to the chamfer top clock described in Chapter Thirteen would be appropriate for this case also. The top of the handle back plate should be set about $\frac{1}{16}$ in (1.5 mm) below the springing of the lancet top.

If larger cases are formed as veneered boxes,

constructors may wish to delete the lancet work beneath the dial and substitute one of the shell or fan inlays sold by veneer suppliers. Decorations of this kind are authentic, but they are not sold in small enough sizes for the clock as detailed.

The comment made in the previous chapter about planing allowances and case depth applies to this clock also. Alternative case dimensions to suit a range of bezel sizes are given in the table.

CLOCK DIMENSION			BEZEL DIAMETERS				
			$3\frac{3}{8}$ & $3\frac{5}{8}$ in 85 & 92 mm	4 in 100 mm	$4\frac{3}{8}$ & $4\frac{1}{2}$ in 110 & 115 mm	$5\frac{1}{8}$ & $5\frac{1}{4}$ in 130 & 135 mm	$5\frac{3}{4}$ & 6 in 145 & 150 mm
H	HEIGHT	in	$8\frac{1}{2}$	$9\frac{1}{4}$	$10\frac{5}{8}$	$12\frac{1}{2}$	$13\frac{7}{8}$
		mm	216	235	270	317	352
W	WIDTH	in	$4\frac{1}{8}$	$4\frac{1}{2}$	$5\frac{1}{8}$	6	$6\frac{3}{4}$
		mm	106	115	131	154	171
D	DEPTH	in	$2\frac{3}{8}$	$2\frac{5}{8}$	3	$3\frac{1}{2}$	4
		mm	60	67	76	89	101
BASE MOULDING		in	$\frac{3}{8} \times \frac{3}{4}$	$\frac{3}{8} \times \frac{13}{16}$	$\frac{7}{16} \times \frac{15}{16}$	$\frac{1}{2} \times 1\frac{1}{8}$	$\frac{5}{8} \times 1\frac{1}{4}$
		mm	9 × 19	9 × 21	11 × 24	13 × 28	16 × 32
FEET diameter × overall height		in	$\frac{3}{4} \times \frac{1}{2}$	$\frac{7}{8} \times \frac{9}{16}$	$1 \times \frac{5}{8}$	$1\frac{1}{8} \times \frac{3}{4}$	$1\frac{1}{4} \times \frac{7}{8}$
		mm	19 × 13	22 × 15	25 × 16	28 × 19	32 × 22

Notes

1 The lancet radius is three-quarters of the case width (see Fig. 80).

2 If caddy feet are fitted, try $\frac{1}{2}$ in (13 mm) diameter items for the first two case sizes, $\frac{3}{4}$ in (19 mm) for the next two and 1 in (25 mm) for the largest size.

3 If ring handles are fitted, use $1\frac{1}{2}$ in (38 mm) diameter items for the first three sizes and 2 in (50 mm) diameter handles for the last two.

The lancet top clock

The Arch Top

Fig 81

HISTORY AND DERIVATION

The lancet top and the arch top were both late eighteenth-century designs, although authorities agree that the lancet top case pre-dates the arch top.

Arch top clocks were often elaborated with finials and a typical example is illustrated in Fig. 82. The arrangement was generally crowned by a pineapple decoration, but if caddy or ball feet were fitted, the finial would usually be terminated by a ball on a stem. The corners of the tapering finial were sometimes rounded to bring the tip to a circular section which aligned with the stem of the decoration.

Pierced brass side panels and ring handles were a common feature and, predictably, the side panels were topped by semicircular arches.

Clocks in this style ranged from about 10 in (250 mm) to 18 in (450 mm) high, excluding any finial.

GENERAL DETAILS OF THE DESIGN

The clock is shown in the photograph on page 95 and in Figs. 81 and 82. The simulated stringing is simpler than that applied to the lancet top and standard scotia is used to form the base moulding.

Choice of Wood

Any of the woods listed for the lancet top can be used for this design, although mahogany and satinwood are particularly authentic choices.

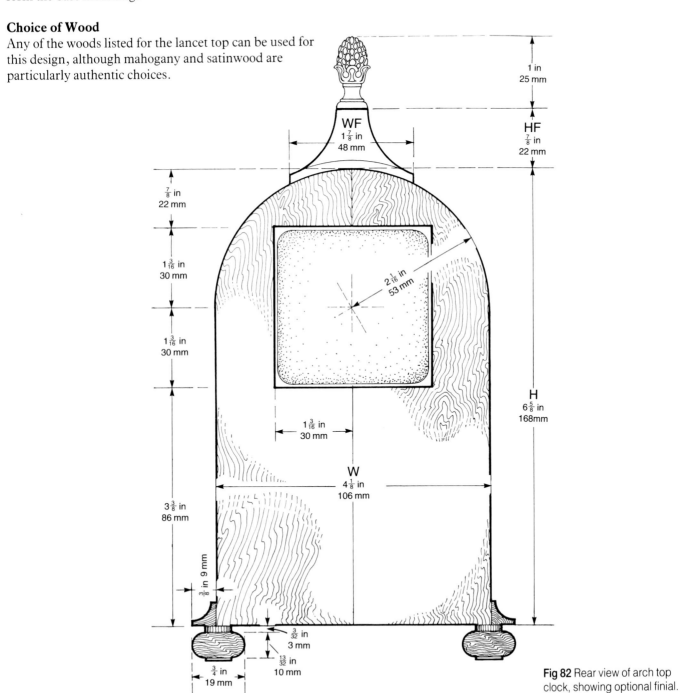

Fig 82 Rear view of arch top clock, showing optional finial.

MATERIALS AND COMPONENTS

Cutting List

- Built-up block case, one off, $15 \times 2\frac{1}{2} \times 2\frac{1}{2}$ in ($380 \times 64 \times 64$ mm)

  or

  One-piece block case, one off, $7\frac{1}{2} \times 4\frac{1}{2} \times 2\frac{1}{2}$ in ($190 \times 115 \times 65$ mm)
- Base mouldings (scotia), out of $12 \times \frac{3}{8} \times \frac{3}{8}$ in ($300 \times 9 \times 9$ mm)
- Bun feet, turned from $9 \times 1 \times 1$ in ($230 \times 25 \times 25$ mm)
- Finial base (if fitted), one off, $2\frac{1}{8} \times 2\frac{1}{8} \times 1\frac{1}{2}$ in ($54 \times 54 \times 38$ mm)
- Movement access flap, $\frac{1}{8}$ in (3 mm) plywood, $3\frac{1}{2} \times 3$ in (90×76 mm)

OTHER MATERIALS AND COMPONENTS

- Quartz movement
- Brass, bezel, complete with domed glass and backing plate, $3\frac{5}{8}$ in (92 mm) diameter
- Hands and card dial
- Five $\frac{3}{8}$ in (9 mm) No. 6 brass screws for securing the dial back plate and the access flap
- Brass pineapple, 1 in (25 mm) high (required only if the finial is fitted)

CONSTRUCTION

The arch top case is probably the simplest of all of the clocks in this collection to construct. The availability of ready-made scotia moulding even eliminates the scratch stock work.

Comments regarding planing allowances and case depth, caddy feet, ring handles and shell or fan inlays made earlier in connection with the lancet top case apply to the arch top case also. Alternative case dimensions to suit a range of bezel sizes are given in the table.

CLOCK DIMENSION			BEZEL DIAMETERS				
			$3\frac{3}{8}$ & $3\frac{5}{8}$ in 85 & 92 mm	4 in 100 mm	$4\frac{3}{8}$ & $4\frac{1}{2}$ in 110 & 115 mm	$5\frac{1}{8}$ & $5\frac{1}{4}$ in 130 & 135 mm	$5\frac{3}{4}$ & 6 in 145 & 150 mm
H	HEIGHT	in	$6\frac{5}{8}$	$7\frac{1}{4}$	$8\frac{1}{4}$	$9\frac{3}{4}$	$10\frac{3}{4}$
		mm	168	184	210	247	274
W	WIDTH	in	$4\frac{1}{8}$	$4\frac{1}{2}$	$5\frac{1}{8}$	6	$6\frac{3}{4}$
		mm	106	115	131	154	171
D	DEPTH	in	$2\frac{3}{8}$	$2\frac{5}{8}$	3	$3\frac{1}{2}$	4
		mm	60	67	76	89	101
HF	HEIGHT OF FINIAL	in	$\frac{7}{8}$	1	$1\frac{1}{8}$	$1\frac{1}{4}$	$1\frac{3}{8}$
		mm	22	25	29	32	35
WF	WIDTH AND DEPTH OF FINIAL	in	$1\frac{7}{8}$	$2\frac{1}{16}$	$2\frac{3}{8}$	$2\frac{3}{4}$	$3\frac{1}{8}$
		mm	48	52	60	70	79
FEET diameter × overall height		in	$\frac{3}{4} \times \frac{1}{2}$	$\frac{7}{8} \times \frac{9}{16}$	$1 \times \frac{5}{8}$	$1\frac{1}{8} \times \frac{3}{4}$	$1\frac{1}{4} \times \frac{7}{8}$
		mm	19 × 13	22 × 15	25 × 16	28 × 19	32 × 22

Notes

1 Use a $\frac{3}{8}$ in (9 mm) scotia as a base moulding for the first two sizes, $\frac{1}{2}$ in (13 mm) for the next two and $\frac{5}{8}$ in (16 mm) for the largest size.

2 Modify the taper on the finial base as necessary, and fit $1\frac{3}{8}$ in (35 mm) pineapples to the last two case sizes if the clock is elaborated in this way.

Two arch top clocks. The version with the finial is in satinwood

CHAPTER THIRTEEN

Three Clocks of the Regency Period

REGENCY AND EMPIRE

The future king of England, George IV, acted as Regent between 1811 and 1820. Greek and Egyptian revival styles fashionable in England between about 1800 and 1830 thus became known as Regency. In France, this period is called Empire.

English interiors and furnishings were influenced by designers Thomas Sheraton and George Smith, the architect Henry Holland and the novelist and philosopher Thomas Hope. Although Smith and Hope did much to popularize the introduction of ancient Egyptian motifs, the art and architecture of the ancient Greeks remained the dominant theme throughout the period.

Apart from an Egyptianized clock in Hope's book, *Household Furniture and Interior Decoration*, these four mentors of fashion did not produce any clock designs, and it was left to the makers of cases to incorporate the revived styles into their work. The result was often a quaint mixture of Greek, Egyptian, Roman and even Gothic elements.

Some nineteenth-century American clocks reveal the influence of the Greek revival. Indeed, the circular cased clock described later is actually listed in E. Ingraham and Co.'s catalogues as their 'Grecian' model.

The Chamfer Top Case

Fig 83 Front view of chamfer top clock.

HISTORY AND DERIVATION

This clock more than any other is associated with the Regency period. Rather obviously, it takes its name from the wide chamfers applied to the top moulding. The pitched-roof form produced by this chamfering, together with the cornice effect of the scotia, are said to show the influence of the Greek revival.

Chamfer topped clocks ranged in size from approximately 10 in (250 mm) to 20 in (500 mm) high, with around 16 in (400 mm) being typical.

The chamfer top clock

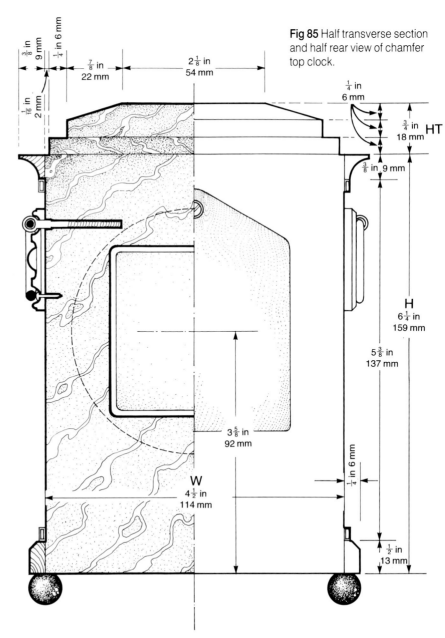

Fig 84 Side view of chamfer top clock: (a) alternative top piece to accommodate pineapple finial.

(a)

GENERAL DETAILS OF THE DESIGN

The clock is shown in the photograph opposite and in Figs. 83, 84 and 85. Stopped chamfers to the front of the case, brass inlay, ring handles and caddy feet were characteristic features of the antique originals. The brass strips adjacent to the scotia and base mouldings are a substitute for the original fluted inlay. Machine-made decoration of this kind would be difficult or impossible to obtain now.

Fig 85 Half transverse section and half rear view of chamfer top clock.

A pineapple finial was often applied, and Fig. 84 illustrates an alternative arrangement for the chamfer top which creates a platform for an ornament of this kind.

Choice of Wood

Mahogany was used more than any other wood for these cases. Rosewood and satinwood would also be appropriate, and ebonized examples are not unknown.

MATERIALS AND COMPONENTS

Cutting List

- Built-up block case, one off, $14 \times 2\frac{1}{2} \times 2\frac{1}{2}$ in ($360 \times 64 \times 64$ mm)
  or
  One-piece block case, one off, $7 \times 5 \times 2\frac{1}{2}$ in ($180 \times 130 \times 65$ mm)
- Chamfer top, out of $10 \times 2\frac{1}{2} \times \frac{1}{4}$ in ($255 \times 65 \times 6$ mm) *finished* thickness strip
- Top moulding (scotia) out of $15 \times \frac{3}{8} \times \frac{3}{8}$ in ($380 \times 9 \times 9$ mm)
- Base moulding, out of $15 \times \frac{1}{4} \times \frac{1}{2}$ in ($380 \times 6 \times 13$ mm)
- Movement access flap, $\frac{1}{8}$ in (3 mm) plywood, $3\frac{1}{2} \times 3$ in (90×76 mm)

OTHER MATERIALS AND COMPONENTS

- Quartz movement
- Brass bezel, complete with domed glass and backing plate, $3\frac{5}{8}$ in (92 mm) diameter
- Hands and card dial
- Brass strip or rectangular section brass tube, $24 \times \frac{3}{32} \times \frac{3}{16}$ in ($610 \times 2 \times 5$ mm)
- Ring handles, two off, $1\frac{1}{2}$ in (38 mm) diameter
- Caddy (ball) feet, four off, $\frac{1}{2}$ in (13 mm) diameter
- Five $\frac{3}{8}$ in (9 mm) No. 6 brass screws for securing the dial back plate and the access flap
- Two brass escutcheon pins (for ring handle back plates)

Note

See the components list in Chapter Six for details of the suppliers of brass tube.

CONSTRUCTION

The case was formed from a built-up block but a box-type construction would be preferable for the larger versions. Because of the corner chamfers, solid hardwood in strip or board form is the preferred material for constructing the box. A $\frac{1}{2} \times \frac{1}{2}$ in (13×13 mm) hardwood lipping, glued to the vertical edges of a veneered plywood front panel, would provide solid wood to cut the chamfers into, but the lipping and the veneer would have to be carefully matched.

Mitre cuts in the brass tube or strip are finished on the disc sander. After the tube has been cut and abraded to a perfect fit, remove any burrs, polish it and coat it with clear cellulose. Balsa cement can then be used to attach the pieces to the case.

Alternative case dimensions to suit a range of bezel sizes are given in the table.

CLOCK DIMENSION			BEZEL DIAMETERS				
			$3\frac{3}{8}$ & $3\frac{5}{8}$ in 85 & 92 mm	4 in 100 mm	$4\frac{3}{8}$ & $4\frac{1}{2}$ in 110 & 115 mm	$5\frac{1}{8}$ & $5\frac{1}{4}$ in 130 & 135 mm	$5\frac{3}{4}$ & 6 in 145 & 150 mm
H	HEIGHT	in	$6\frac{1}{4}$	$6\frac{7}{8}$	$7\frac{7}{8}$	$9\frac{1}{4}$	$10\frac{1}{4}$
		mm	159	174	200	235	260
W	WIDTH	in	$4\frac{1}{2}$	$4\frac{7}{8}$	$5\frac{5}{8}$	$6\frac{5}{8}$	$7\frac{3}{8}$
		mm	114	124	143	168	187
D	DEPTH	in	$2\frac{3}{8}$	$2\frac{5}{8}$	3	$3\frac{1}{2}$	$3\frac{7}{8}$
		mm	60	67	76	89	98
HT	HEIGHT OF TOP	in	$\frac{3}{4}$	$\frac{27}{32}$	$\frac{15}{16}$	$1\frac{1}{8}$	$1\frac{7}{32}$
		mm	18	21	24	27	30
COVE MOULDING		in	$\frac{3}{8} \times \frac{3}{8}$	$\frac{3}{8} \times \frac{3}{8}$	$\frac{1}{2} \times \frac{1}{2}$	$\frac{1}{2} \times \frac{1}{2}$	$\frac{5}{8} \times \frac{5}{8}$
		mm	9×9	9×9	13×13	13×13	16
BASE MOULDING		in	$\frac{1}{4} \times \frac{1}{2}$	$\frac{1}{4} \times \frac{9}{16}$	$\frac{5}{16} \times \frac{5}{8}$	$\frac{5}{16} \times \frac{3}{4}$	$\frac{3}{8} \times \frac{7}{8}$
		mm	6×13	6×14	8×16	8×19	9×22
BRASS STRIP		in	$\frac{3}{32} \times \frac{3}{16}$	$\frac{3}{32} \times \frac{3}{16}$	$\frac{1}{8} \times \frac{1}{4}$	$\frac{1}{8} \times \frac{1}{4}$	$\frac{5}{32} \times \frac{5}{16}$
		mm	2.5×5	2.5×5	3×6	3×6	4×8
CADDY FEET		in	$\frac{1}{2}$	$\frac{1}{2}$	$\frac{3}{4}$	$\frac{3}{4}$	1
		mm	13	13	19	19	25

Note

1 The specified ring handles can be used for the first two sizes of case, but 2 in (50 mm) diameter handles should be fitted to the remaining three sizes.

Fig 86 Front view of circular cased clock.

Circular Cased Clock

HISTORY AND DERIVATION

Probably of French origin, this type of case was popular in England and France during the first three decades of the eighteenth century. In America, the influence of the Greek revival was more prolonged and clocks of this kind were manufactured by E. Ingraham and Co. of Bristol, Connecticut, into the 1880s. They also produced a mosaic version by building up the turning blank for the circular case or drum from different coloured woods.

On high-quality cases, volutes were carved into the cylinders beneath the drum, making the support for the clock resemble more closely a Greek Ionic capital. American and other manufacturers simplified this decoration into concentric rings, which could be cut on a lathe.

E. Ingraham and Co.'s so-called 'Grecian model' was 14½ in (368 mm) high. European versions ranged in height from about 9 in (230 mm) to 15 in (380 mm).

The circular cased clock. American
clockmaker E. Ingraham gave the name
'Grecian' to cases of this kind

GENERAL DETAILS OF THE DESIGN

The case is shown in the photograph opposite and in Figs. 86, 87, 88, 89 and 90. With lathe-cut decorations on the cylinder ends it has more in common with the Grecian clock manufactured by E. Ingraham than with the French Empire examples. Square feet were fitted to this case, but bun feet were also common. If these are preferred, the range of sizes suggested for the lancet and arch top cases would be suitable.

Choice of Wood

Mahogany, rosewood and satinwood are all appropriate, but cedar of Lebanon was chosen because it works and turns very easily to a good finish, and excessive demands are not made on the lathe, despite the diameter of the case. Pronounced growth rings add interest to the turnings, especially if orientated as shown in Fig. 89.

MATERIALS AND COMPONENTS

Cutting List

Turning blanks:
- For the case, one off, $4\frac{3}{4} \times 4\frac{3}{4} \times 2\frac{3}{4}$ in ($120 \times 120 \times 70$ mm)
- For the cylinders, two off, out of $6 \times 1\frac{3}{4} \times 1\frac{3}{4}$ in ($152 \times 44 \times 44$ mm)
- For the cylinder ends, two off, out of $3\frac{1}{2} \times 1\frac{3}{4} \times 1$ in ($90 \times 44 \times 25$ mm)

The following out of $\frac{3}{8}$ in (9 mm) *finished* thickness material:
- Stand front and back, two off, $5 \times 2\frac{1}{4}$ in (127×57 mm)
- Base front, one off, $6\frac{1}{4} \times 1\frac{3}{4}$ in (160×45 mm)
- Base rear, one off, $5\frac{1}{2} \times 1\frac{3}{4}$ in (140×45 mm)
- Base sides, two off, $3\frac{1}{4} \times 1\frac{3}{4}$ in (83×45 mm)
- Base bottom, one off, $5\frac{1}{2} \times 2\frac{1}{4}$ in (140×57 mm)

- Base top from $\frac{1}{4}$ in (6 mm) *finished* thickness material, one off, $5\frac{1}{2} \times 2\frac{3}{4}$ in (140×70 mm)
- Feet, four off, out of $5 \times 1 \times \frac{1}{4}$ in ($127 \times 25 \times 6$ mm)
- Stand side pieces from scrap
- Scotia mouldings, out of $15 \times \frac{3}{8} \times \frac{3}{8}$ in ($380 \times 9 \times 9$ mm)
- Quadrant mouldings, out of $15 \times \frac{1}{4} \times \frac{1}{4}$ in ($380 \times 6 \times 6$ mm)
- Movement access disc, out of $\frac{1}{8}$ in (3 mm) plywood $4\frac{1}{2} \times 4\frac{1}{2}$ in (114×114 mm)

Fig 87 Section through circular cased clock.

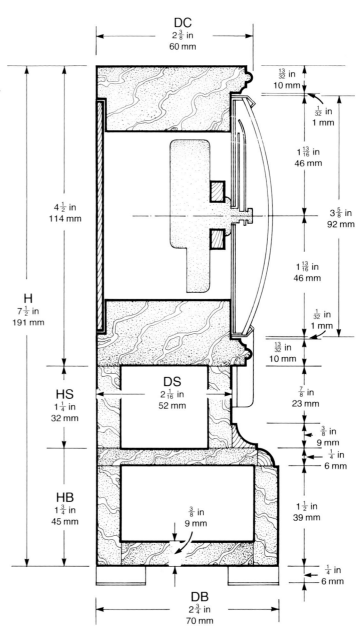

Egyptian Revival Clock

HISTORY AND DERIVATION

The earliest revival of the Egyptian style was during the reign of the Roman emperor Hadrian; the most recent during the 1920s, inspired by the discovery of Tutankhamun's tomb. It is, however, the eighteenth-century revival that concerns us here. Stimulated by Napoleon's Egyptian campaigns, it went on to influence the decorative arts during the English Regency and French Empire periods.

In 1769, the Italian artist and architect Piranesi published a volume of engravings which included interiors in the ancient Egyptian style. Percier and Fontaine, Napoleon's favourite architects, likewise included Egyptianized furniture and pylon-form clocks in a collection of designs they published in 1812. It is likely that Thomas Hope drew on these sources for his own book on interior decoration. A clock made to his design, with the dial held by a figure of the goddess Isis and flanked by obelisks decorated with hieroglyphs, is displayed in Brighton at the Royal Pavilion. This version, which does not have the moon disc head-dress depicted on Hope's drawings, is $20\frac{1}{2}$ in (520 mm) tall, with a 4 in (100 mm) diameter bezel and Gothic Roman numerals on the dial.

Pylon-form mantel clocks of the Regency period were about 11 in (280 mm) to 20 in (500 mm) tall, excluding any pineapple finials.

Decorated and plain versions of the Egyptian revival clock

GENERAL DETAILS OF THE DESIGN

Carving realistic figures is beyond the skill of most amateur (and many professional) craftsmen, and this design relies on ancient Egyptian architectural forms to achieve the desired effect. Two versions are included, one plain and one decorated, and they are shown in the photographs on page 107 and in Figs. 91, 92, 93, 94 and 95.

The case is in the form of a pylon surmounted by a typical gorge and roll moulding (the deepened scotia and

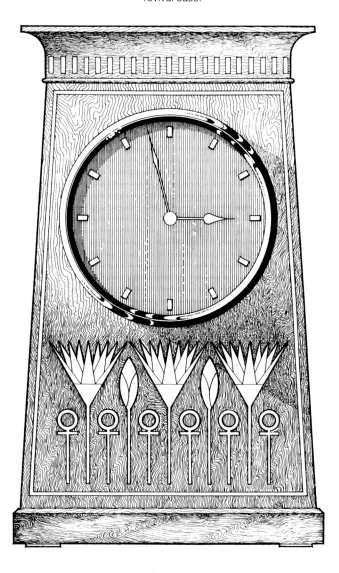

Fig 91 Front view of Egyptian revival case.

narrow bead that crown the clock). A chamfered base moulding enhances the feeling of solidity and it should be noted that the base moulding is vertical where it returns around the sides of the case.

Pylons, the towers which flanked the entrances to Egyptian temples, had all four faces battered, but only the sides of the case are raked. This is sufficient to create the desired effect, eases construction and avoids the viewing problems associated with a mantel clock that has its face inclined upwards.

Choice of Wood

Again, mahogany, rosewood or satinwood are all appropriate. Constructors who do not mind using soft-woods might care to try pine or cedar of Lebanon. (The ancient Egyptians imported these timbers, along with cypress, yew and ebony.)

MATERIALS AND COMPONENTS

Cutting List

The following out of $\frac{3}{8}$ in (9 mm) *finished* thickness material:
- Front and back of case, two off, $5\frac{1}{4} \times 7\frac{1}{2}$ in (134 × 190 mm)
- Sides of case, two off, $2\frac{1}{2} \times 7\frac{1}{2}$ in (64 × 190 mm)
- Bottom of case, one off, $5\frac{1}{4} \times 3\frac{1}{4}$ in (134 × 83 mm)
- Top of case, one off, $4\frac{1}{8} \times 3\frac{1}{8}$ in (105 × 80 mm)

Strips, in the following *finished* sizes:
- Gorge (scotia), out of $18 \times \frac{5}{8} \times \frac{5}{8}$ in (460 × 16 × 16 mm)
- Gorge extension, out of $18 \times \frac{3}{16} \times \frac{3}{8}$ in (460 × 5 × 9 mm)
- Roll, out of $18 \times \frac{1}{2} \times \frac{1}{8}$ in (460 × 13 × 3 mm)
- Base mouldings, out of $18 \times \frac{1}{8} \times \frac{3}{4}$ in (460 × 3 × 19 mm)
- Top packing pieces, out of $18 \times \frac{3}{8} \times \frac{5}{8}$ in (460 × 9 × 16 mm)
- Movement access flap, one off, $\frac{1}{8}$ in (3 mm) plywood, $3\frac{1}{2} \times 3$ in (90 × 76 mm)

OTHER MATERIALS AND COMPONENTS

- Quartz movement
- Brass bezel, complete with domed glass and backing plate, $3\frac{5}{8}$ in (92 mm) diameter
- Hands and card dial or dial-making materials (see Chapter Five); fit a Roman numeral dial with spade or

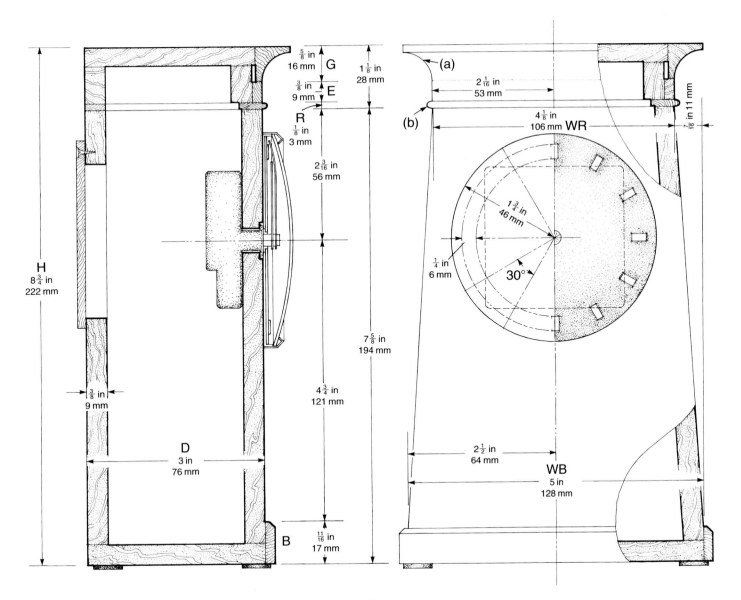

Fig 92 Section through Egyptian revival case.

Fig 93 Dial and constructional details of Egyptian revival case: (a) gorge; (b) roll.

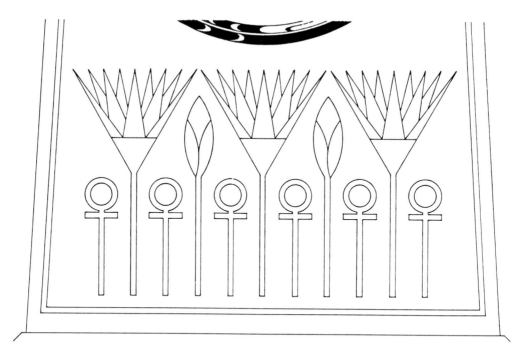

Fig 94 Full-size details of
decoration to Egyptian revival case.

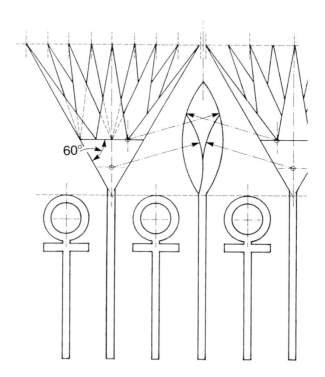

Fig 95 Setting-out details of
decoration to Egyptian revival case.

cathedral hands to plain versions of the clock

- Five $\frac{3}{8}$ in (9 mm) No. 6 brass screws for securing the dial back plate and the access flap

If $\frac{3}{8}$ or $\frac{1}{2}$ in (9 or 13 mm) plywood is used to construct the case, a short leaf of veneer, 36×6 in (920×152 mm) will be required.

CONSTRUCTION

This case is complicated by the taper and by the way the gorge and roll mouldings have to sit on top of the basic box instead of being wrapped around it. Guidance given in Chapter Three still holds good, but the following additional suggestions may prove helpful.

① Plane the front and back panels true and square and initially to a rectangular shape $\frac{1}{16}$ in (1.5 mm) wider than the finished base width. Mark out the centre lines, mark out the splay, then clamp the pieces together in the vice and plane down to the splay lines, removing the $\frac{1}{16}$ in excess in the process. Construction of the box can then proceed as described earlier.

② Glue the bottom panel in position, then mark the height of the base moulding on the case and plane the case sides vertical below this line.

③ Glue the $\frac{3}{8}$ in (9 mm) strip to the scotia to form the deep gorge moulding. Select unblemished pieces, and cramp them together with four 2 in (50 mm) G cramps. If this is done carefully the joint will be imperceptible after a light sanding.

④ Round the edge of the $\frac{1}{2} \times \frac{1}{8}$ in (13×3 mm) strip to form the roll, cut and mitre the pieces and glue them in position on top of the case.

⑤ Cut and mitre the pieces of the gorge moulding and glue them in position on top of the roll. Because of their shape, they will have to be held by hand until the initial set of the glue takes place.

⑥ Glue the back filler pieces and top supports in place. Plane the top to a tight fit, then glue it in position.

⑦ If the case is veneered, lay the veneer to the front and sides before gluing the mouldings in position. It is best to veneer the top piece before it is glued in place, so that the top of the scotia can remain exposed as a mitred border.

The procedure for decorating the case is fully described in Chapter Four. Alternative case dimensions for a range of bezel sizes are given in the table.

CLOCK DIMENSION			BEZEL DIAMETERS				
			$3\frac{3}{8}$ & $3\frac{5}{8}$ in 85 & 92 mm	4 in 100 mm	$4\frac{3}{8}$ & $4\frac{1}{2}$ in 110 & 115 mm	$5\frac{1}{8}$ & $5\frac{1}{4}$ in 130 & 135 mm	$5\frac{3}{4}$ & 6 in 145 & 150 mm
H	HEIGHT	in	$8\frac{3}{4}$	$9\frac{1}{2}$	11	$12\frac{7}{8}$	$14\frac{1}{4}$
		mm	222	241	279	326	362
WR	WIDTH AT ROLL	in	$4\frac{1}{8}$	$4\frac{1}{2}$	$5\frac{1}{8}$	6	$6\frac{3}{4}$
		mm	106	114	130	152	171
WB	WIDTH AT BASE	in	5	$5\frac{7}{16}$	$6\frac{1}{4}$	$7\frac{1}{4}$	$8\frac{1}{8}$
		mm	128	138	159	184	206
D	DEPTH	in	3	$3\frac{1}{4}$	$3\frac{3}{4}$	$4\frac{1}{2}$	$4\frac{7}{8}$
		mm	76	83	95	114	124
G	GORGE	in	$\frac{5}{8}$	$\frac{5}{8}$	$\frac{3}{4}$	$\frac{7}{8}$	1
		mm	16	16	19	22	25
E	GORGE EXTENSION	in	$\frac{3}{8}$	$\frac{3}{8}$	$\frac{1}{2}$	$\frac{1}{2}$	$\frac{5}{8}$
		mm	9	9	13	13	16
R	ROLL	in	$\frac{1}{8}$	$\frac{1}{8}$	$\frac{1}{8}$	$\frac{3}{16}$	$\frac{3}{16}$
		mm	3	3	3	4.5	4.5
B	BASE MOULDING	in	$\frac{1}{8} \times \frac{11}{16}$	$\frac{1}{8} \times \frac{3}{4}$	$\frac{5}{32} \times \frac{7}{8}$	$\frac{3}{16} \times 1$	$\frac{1}{4} \times 1\frac{1}{8}$
		mm	3×17	3×19	4×22	5×25	6×28

CHAPTER FOURTEEN

Pendule d'Officier and Two Carriage Clocks

HISTORY AND DERIVATION

Most horologists agree that the true precursor of the carriage clock was the pendule d'officier.

Ornate high-relief decoration, a round dial occupying the entire front of the case and an upswept finial terminating in the carrying handle combine to give these clocks their distinctive appearance. They were made in France, Germany and Switzerland between about 1780 and 1820, and became known as officers' clocks because of their popularity during the Napoleonic wars.

The Frenchman Abraham-Louis Breguet originated the carriage clock around 1800. His early models had plain wooden cases with bun feet, a carrying handle and a circular white dial in a metal bezel. A decade later, the Swiss Cugnier Leschot was producing carriage clocks in cases that were almost identical to those made by Breguet. Benjamin Louis Vulliamy was probably the first English maker of carriage clocks and he too installed all of his early models in wooden cases. Presumably this was done to reduce weight. It was Paul Garnier who later founded the French carriage clock industry and began producing timepieces in the brass-framed, glass-panelled cases which are now so familiar.

Pendules des officiers and early carriage clocks were usually between 8 in (200 mm) and 9 in (230 mm) tall, including the handle. Burr walnut, rosewood and mahogany were used for the carriage clock cases. Pendules des officiers had cases of gilded brass (ormolu).

The pendule d'officier

Pendule d'Officier

GENERAL DETAILS OF THE DESIGN

The clock is shown in the photograph on page 113 and in Figs. 96, 97, 98 and 99. Its shape and form are closely modelled on a timepiece made by Cugnier Leschot around 1780. Simulated stringing has been substituted for the laurel wreaths which decorated the original case beneath the dial and on the finial. Lion's heads within a framing of simulated stringing take the place of the pateras or floral bosses which embellished the sides; and the lion's-paw bracket feet were very typical of clocks of this kind.

Choice of Wood

This is an interpretation in wood of a metal case and there can be no authentic choice other than to select a species that was popular at the end of the eighteenth century. Honduras mahogany was used, the dark wood contrasting well with the simulated inlay and brass decoration.

Fig 96 Front view of pendule d'officier.

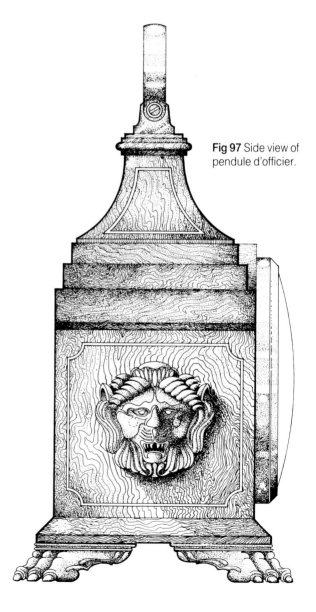

Fig 97 Side view of pendule d'officier.

MATERIALS AND COMPONENTS

Cutting List

The following out of $\frac{3}{8}$ in (9 mm) *finished* thickness material:

- Case front, one off, $3\frac{1}{2} \times 4$ in (90 × 102 mm)
- Sides, two off, $3\frac{1}{4} \times 4$ in (83 × 102 mm)
- Bottom, one off, $3\frac{1}{2} \times 3$ in (90 × 76 mm)
- Rear door, one off, $3\frac{1}{2} \times 3\frac{1}{2}$ in (90 × 90 mm)
- Stepped top, two off, $4\frac{1}{4} \times 3$ in (108 × 76 mm)
- Back fillet, one off, $3\frac{1}{2} \times \frac{1}{4}$ in (90 × 6 mm)

- Finial block, one off, $3\frac{1}{2} \times 2\frac{3}{4} \times 1\frac{3}{4}$ in (90 × 70 × 45 mm)

Strips, in the following *finished* sizes:

- Finial cap, one off, $2 \times \frac{7}{8} \times \frac{1}{8}$ in (50 × 22 × 3 mm)
- Finial bead, out of $9 \times \frac{1}{8} \times \frac{1}{4}$ in (230 × 3 × 6 mm)
- Shoulder mouldings, out of $9 \times \frac{3}{16} \times \frac{5}{8}$ in (230 × 5 × 16 mm)
- Base mouldings, out of $21 \times \frac{1}{4} \times \frac{3}{8}$ in (530 × 6 × 9 mm)
- Packing piece behind top of dial, one off, $4 \times \frac{1}{4} \times \frac{3}{4}$ in (102 × 6 × 19 mm)
- Door stop lath, one off, $4 \times \frac{1}{8} \times \frac{1}{8}$ in (102 × 3 × 3 mm)

OTHER MATERIALS AND COMPONENTS

- Quartz movement
- Brass bezel, complete with domed glass and back plate, $3\frac{5}{8}$ in (92 mm) diameter
- Hands and card dial
- Four $\frac{3}{8}$ in (9 mm) No. 4 brass screws for securing the dial back plate
- Handle, $2\frac{1}{8} \times 1\frac{3}{8}$ in high (54 × 35 mm)
- Lion's heads, $1\frac{1}{4}$ in (45 mm) diameter
- Lion's-paw feet, $1\frac{3}{8} \times 1\frac{3}{8}$ in (35 × 35 mm)
- Brass screws and pins for securing brassware
- Pair of $\frac{3}{4}$ in (19 mm) brass hinges, complete with brass screws
- Brass hook-and-eye fastener for rear door

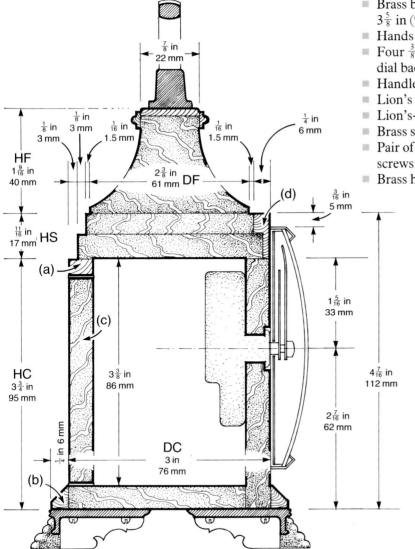

Fig 98 Section through pendule d'officier: (a) fillet at top of door; (b) base moulding carried around back of case; (c) movement access door; (d) curved packing piece behind top of dial.

Note

Lion's heads without rings are required for this clock. If difficulty is encountered, remove the rings from heads equipped in this way and plug the holes with brass rod cut from screw shanks.

CONSTRUCTION

The sides of the case overlap the front panel and the cutting list allows for this. (The joints are masked by the dial and simulated stringing.)

Rough-cut the finial with a coping or bow saw and carve, file and then sand it to the required profile. Form

the rebate in the packing piece behind the top of the dial and finish it to a snug fit around the stepped top before rounding it on the disc sander.

Ideally, the handle fixing bolts should extend to the inside of the case. If they are not long enough, tighten them into the handle and embed them in epoxy-resin-filled holes in the finial.

The table gives key dimensions for two alternative bezel sizes, one or the other of which should be obtainable worldwide. Difficulty would probably be encountered in obtaining suitable decorative brassware for larger versions of the case.

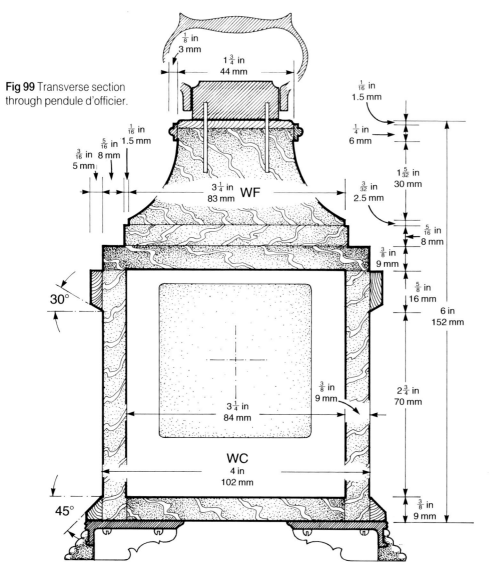

Fig 99 Transverse section through pendule d'officier.

	CLOCK DIMENSION		BEZEL DIAMETERS	
			$3\frac{5}{8}$ in 92mm	4 in 100mm
HC	HEIGHT OF CASE	in mm	$3\frac{3}{4}$ 95	$4\frac{1}{16}$ 103
WC	WIDTH OF CASE	in mm	4 102	$4\frac{3}{8}$ 111
DC	DEPTH OF CASE	in mm	3 76	$3\frac{1}{4}$ 83
HS	HEIGHT OF STEPS	in mm	$\frac{11}{16}$ 17	$\frac{3}{4}$ 19
HF	HEIGHT OF FINIAL	in mm	$1\frac{9}{16}$ 40	$1\frac{3}{4}$ 44
WF	WIDTH OF FINIAL	in mm	$3\frac{1}{4}$ 83	$3\frac{1}{2}$ 90
DF	DEPTH OF FINIAL	in mm	$2\frac{3}{8}$ 61	$2\frac{1}{2}$ 65

Note

1 Keep the shoulder and base mouldings a shaving or two larger than the dimensions given on the drawing when constructing the larger case.

Round Dial Carriage Clock

Fig 100 Front view of round dial carriage clock. Case width is 4 in (102 mm).

GENERAL DETAILS OF THE DESIGN

Although inspired by the early wooden carriage clocks of Breguet and Leschot, bold top and base mouldings impart a vigour to this design which is absent from the very austere originals. The clock is shown in the photograph on page 121 and in Figs. 100 and 101. A full-size section of

the mouldings is given in Fig. 104. Tinted varnish was used to match the bezel to the antique handle. This technique is described in Chapter Five.

Choice of Wood
Pine was used for this case, but the woods used by Breguet and Leschot would be more authentic.

MATERIALS AND COMPONENTS

Cutting List

The following out of $\frac{3}{8}$ in (9 mm) *finished* thickness material:

- Front and back, two off, $4\frac{1}{4} \times 6\frac{1}{4}$ in (108 × 160 mm)
- Sides, two off, $2 \times 6\frac{1}{4}$ in (51 × 160 mm)
- Top and bottom, two off, $2\frac{3}{4} \times 4\frac{1}{4}$ in (70 × 108 mm)

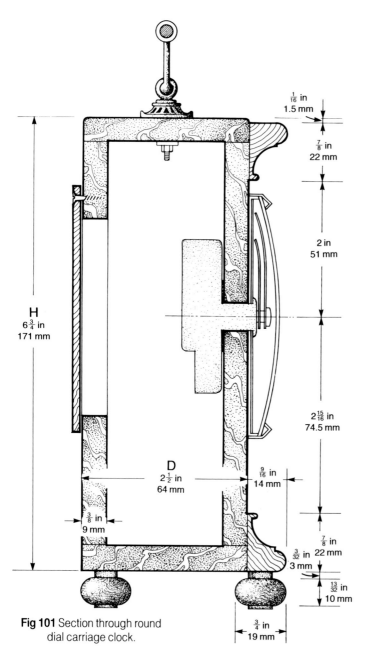

Fig 101 Section through round dial carriage clock.

Strips, in the following *finished* sizes:

- Mouldings, out of $30 \times \frac{9}{16} \times \frac{7}{8}$ in (760 × 14 × 22 mm)
- Feet, four off, out of $9 \times 1 \times 1$ in (230 × 25 × 25 mm)
- Movement access flap, $\frac{1}{8}$ in (3 mm) plywood, $3\frac{1}{2} \times 3$ in (90 × 76 mm)

OTHER MATERIALS AND COMPONENTS

- Quartz movement
- Brass bezel, complete with domed glass and backing plate, $3\frac{5}{8}$ in (92 mm) diameter
- Hands and card dial
- Five $\frac{3}{8}$ in (9 mm) No. 6 brass screws for securing the dial back plate and the access flap
- Handle, $2\frac{3}{8}$ in (60 mm) fixing centres

CONSTRUCTION

This is a simple box-type case and nothing needs to be added to the guidance given in Chapter Three. Turn the bun feet from ramin or sycamore if pine is used for the case.

Alternative case dimensions for a range of bezel sizes are given in the table.

CLOCK DIMENSION			BEZEL DIAMETERS		
			$3\frac{3}{8}$ & $3\frac{5}{8}$ in 85 & 92 mm	4 in 100 mm	$4\frac{3}{8}$ & $4\frac{1}{2}$ in 110 & 115 mm
H	HEIGHT	in	$6\frac{3}{4}$	$7\frac{1}{4}$	$8\frac{1}{2}$
		mm	171	184	216
W	WIDTH	in	4	$4\frac{3}{8}$	5
		mm	102	111	127
D	DEPTH	in	$2\frac{1}{2}$	$2\frac{3}{4}$	$3\frac{1}{4}$
		mm	64	70	83
MOULDING		in	$\frac{9}{16} \times \frac{7}{8}$	$\frac{9}{16} \times \frac{7}{8}$	$\frac{11}{16} \times 1\frac{1}{8}$
		mm	14 × 22	14 × 22	18 × 29
FEET diameter × overall height		in	$\frac{3}{4} \times \frac{1}{2}$	$\frac{7}{8} \times \frac{9}{16}$	$1 \times \frac{5}{8}$
		mm	19 × 13	22 × 14	25 × 16

Notes

1 The moulding on the largest case is becoming too big to be worked easily with the scratch stock, and consideration should be given to building it up in three pieces, perhaps with a standard $\frac{1}{2}$ in (13 mm) machine cut scotia for the centre section.

2 Use the specified handle for the smaller case, a 3 in (76 mm) handle for the medium-size case and a $3\frac{1}{2}$ (89 mm) handle for the largest case.

Glass-fronted Carriage Clock

GENERAL DETAILS OF THE DESIGN

This case is modelled fairly closely on Vulliamy's early carriage clocks. The profile of the top moulding is the same as that used for the round dial carriage clock and is bolder than those applied by Vulliamy. Vulliamy's cases had a stepped capping piece, which could be slid back to reveal the escapement: this feature has been omitted.

Alternative versions of the case are shown in the photograph on page 121. One is in mahogany with brass-covered glazing beads; the other is in pine, with ebonized beads. Construction is detailed in Figs. 102 and 103, and full-size sections through the mouldings are given in Fig. 104.

Choice of Wood

Vulliamy used mahogany or rosewood veneer for his carriage clock cases, and satinwood, also popular during the Regency period, would be appropriate.

MATERIALS AND COMPONENTS

Cutting List

The following out of $\frac{3}{8}$ in (9 mm) *finished* thickness material:

- Sides, two off, $3\frac{1}{8} \times 6\frac{1}{2}$ in (80 × 165 mm)
- Top and bottom, two off, $4\frac{3}{8} \times 3\frac{1}{8}$ in (111 × 80 mm)
- Rear door and dial board, two off, $3\frac{5}{8} \times 6\frac{1}{2}$ in (92 × 165 mm)

Strips, in the following *finished* sizes:

- Top mouldings, out of $18 \times \frac{9}{16} \times \frac{7}{8}$ in (460 × 14 × 22 mm)
- Outer glazing beads, out of $21 \times \frac{1}{8} \times \frac{1}{8}$ in (530 × 3 × 3 mm)
- Inner glazing bead and door stop lath, out of $27 \times \frac{5}{16} \times \frac{1}{8}$ in (690 × 8 × 3 mm)
- Top packing piece, one off, $4 \times \frac{9}{16} \times \frac{3}{4}$ in (102 × 14 × 19 mm)
- Bottom packing piece, one off, $4 \times \frac{9}{16} \times \frac{1}{2}$ in (102 × 14 × 12.5 mm)

Base moulding built up from:

- Scotia, one off, $18 \times \frac{3}{8} \times \frac{3}{8}$ in (460 × 9 × 9 mm) *and*
- Strip, one off, $18 \times \frac{1}{2} \times \frac{3}{4}$ in (460 × 13 × 19 mm)

Fig 102 Front view of glass-fronted carriage clock. The dial card is decorated with rub-down transfers. Case width is $4\frac{1}{8}$ in (105 mm).

OTHER MATERIALS AND COMPONENTS

- Quartz movement
- Hands and card dial
- White card to cover internal glazing bead
- Brass strip for movement fixing brackets, $3 \times \frac{3}{4} \times .032$ in ($76 \times 19 \times 0.8$ mm)
- Four $\frac{1}{4}$ in (6 mm) No. 4 screws for securing the brackets
- Four $\frac{1}{2}$ in (13 mm) No. 6 screws for retaining the dial board

- Pair of $\frac{3}{4}$ in (19 mm) brass hinges complete with screws
- Hook-and-eye fastener, $\frac{3}{4}$ in (19 mm)
- Brass swan-neck cabinet handle, 3 in (76 mm)
- Glass
- Brass angle, two off, $12 \times \frac{5}{32} \times \frac{5}{32}$ in ($305 \times 4 \times 4$ mm)

Notes

- Rectangular brass handles were fitted by Vulliamy, but they are not so readily available in such a wide range of sizes as the swan-neck type.

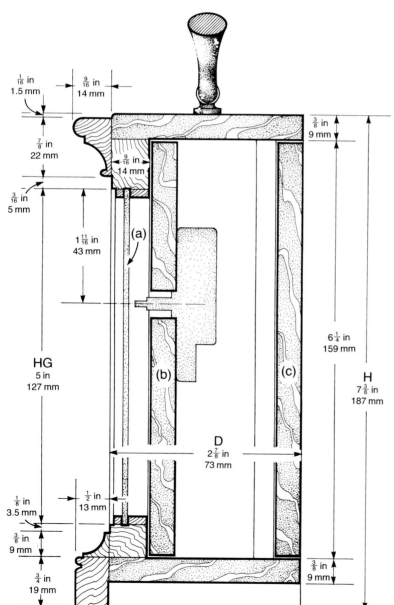

Fig 103 Section through glass-fronted carriage clock:
(a) glass; (b) dial board; (c) rear door.

CLOCK DIMENSION			TIME-RING DIAMETER		
			$2\frac{3}{4}$ in 70 mm	3 in 76 mm	4 in 102 m
H	HEIGHT	in	$7\frac{3}{8}$	$7\frac{3}{4}$	$10\frac{5}{8}$
		mm	187	197	270
HG	HEIGHT OF GLASS	in	5	$5\frac{3}{8}$	$7\frac{1}{4}$
		mm	127	136	184
W	WIDTH	in	$4\frac{1}{8}$	$4\frac{3}{8}$	6
		mm	105	111	152
D	DEPTH	in	$2\frac{7}{8}$	3	$4\frac{1}{4}$
		mm	73	76	108
TOP MOULDING		in	$\frac{9}{16} \times \frac{7}{8}$	$\frac{9}{16} \times \frac{7}{8}$	$\frac{3}{4} \times 1\frac{1}{4}$
		mm	14×22	14×22	19×32
BOTTOM MOULDING		in	$\frac{1}{2} \times 1\frac{1}{8}$	$\frac{1}{2} \times 1\frac{1}{8}$	$\frac{3}{4} \times 1\frac{5}{8}$
		mm	13×28	13×28	19×41
GLAZING BEAD		in	$\frac{1}{8} \times \frac{1}{8}$	$\frac{1}{8} \times \frac{1}{8}$	$\frac{3}{16} \times \frac{3}{16}$
		mm	3×3	3×3	4.5×4.5
SIDE THICKNESS		in	$\frac{3}{8}$	$\frac{3}{8}$	$\frac{1}{2}$
		mm	9	9	13

Note

1 The specified 3 in (76 mm) handle will suit the first two sizes. The largest case requires a 4 in (102 mm) handle.

■ The brass angle is required only if the glazing beads are to be brass-covered. See Chapter Six for details of suppliers.

CONSTRUCTION

Because of the chamfers to the front corners, this case is best constructed from solid wood. If veneered ply must be used, fix a $\frac{3}{8} \times \frac{3}{8}$ in (9 × 9 mm) lipping to the front edge of the side sheets and cut the chamfers into this. Veneer the ply before attaching the lipping, which should be a good match with the veneer.

If the glazing beads are to be ebonized, sanding-seal them with french polish and apply two or three coats of artists' black acrylic colour after they have been cut and disc-sanded to size. Do not use spirit-based dye or stain as it will bleed. Fix the beads in position after the case has been stained and polished.

If brass angle is to be fixed over the beads, perfect the mitres in the angle and abrade it to the exact lengths on the

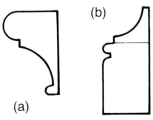

Fig 104 Full-size section through carriage clock mouldings: (a) top and bottom moulding for round dial clock and top moulding for glass-fronted clock; (b) bottom moulding for glass-fronted clock.

disc-sander. Polish it, coat it with clear cellulose and glue it in position on top of the bead, after the case has been stained and polished. Fix the outer glazing beads first and glue white card to the inner beads before gluing them in position.

Alternative case dimensions for a range of time-ring diameters are given in the table. The largest case exceeds the size of Vulliamy's early carriage clocks, but some constructors may wish to build a larger version in this style. If a rectangular card dial cannot be obtained, build one up as described in Chapter Five.

Round dial carriage clock in pine, and pine and mahogany versions of the glass-fronted carriage clock

121

CHAPTER FIFTEEN

Two American Clocks

English case styles prevailed in America until the newly independent nation moved into the nineteenth century. American clockmakers then began developing designs of their own and introduced intensive mass-production techniques to the industry. By 1850, they were exporting thousands of cheap, reliable and distinctively styled clocks. American energy, ingenuity and resourcefulness had brought clock ownership within the reach of ordinary households.

Pillar and Scroll Clock

HISTORY AND DERIVATION

With its high, swan-neck pediment, slender Tuscan columns and urn finials there is just a hint of Hepplewhite's influence on what is considered to be the most inspired and elegant of all American clock cases. The design is widely attributed to Connecticut clockmaker Eli Terry, but it has been suggested that Terry patented only the movement and that the case design was, in fact, the property of Heman Clark and was then pirated by Chauncey Jerome, who was in charge of Terry's case-making operations when the clock was first put into production.

All of this is conjecture. What is important to the craftsman is the case itself, thousands of which were manufactured until its popularity waned towards the end of the 1820s. Described as a shelf clock, it relied on a movement which could be installed in a very shallow case. The originals were usually about 31 in (790 mm) high overall, and generally no more than 5 in (125 mm) deep measured over the plinth. This design is half-size, but case depth has been maintained in the interests of the stability and appearance of what is now a mantel or table clock rather than a shelf-mounted timepiece.

Fig 105 Front view of pillar and scroll clock.

GENERAL DETAILS OF THE DESIGN

The clock is shown in the photographs on page 54 and below, and in Figs. 105, 106, 107 and 108. Individual makers varied the details and general proportions of the case slightly, but the design included here is very typical of the basic pillar and scroll timepieces produced by workshops in Connecticut.

Urn finials on the original antiques were invariably of brass, but wooden turnings were mounted on this scaled-down version because brassware of the correct shape and size is not readily available in the United Kingdom. American constructors are more fortunate: at least one supplier lists urns in a range of sizes, from 1 in (25 mm) to $4\frac{1}{2}$ in (114 mm) high (American suppliers will usually

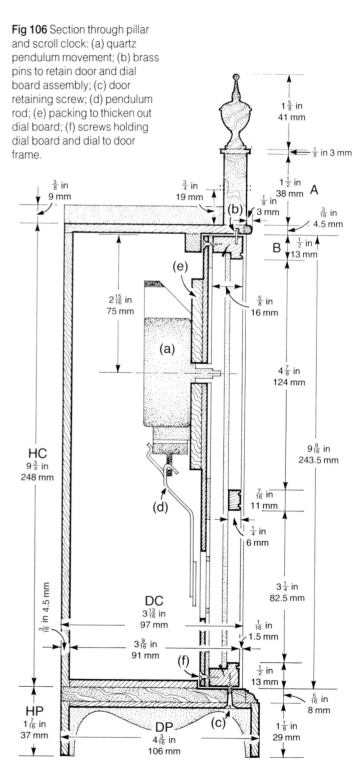

Fig 106 Section through pillar and scroll clock: (a) quartz pendulum movement; (b) brass pins to retain door and dial board assembly; (c) door retaining screw; (d) pendulum rod; (e) packing to thicken out dial board; (f) screws holding dial board and dial to door frame.

The case with the door and dial board assembly removed

export). In the United Kingdom, suitable urns are available for full-size versions of the clock.

A method of simulating pictorial or other decoration to the spandrels and the tablet is suggested in Chapter Five. All of the case sizes tabled allow for a visible margin of mounting card $\frac{7}{16}$ in (11 mm) wide around the dials, with the exception of the full-size version, which includes a $\frac{1}{8}$ in (3 mm) clearance between the time-ring and the door stiles. It has been assumed that constructors building true replicas will adopt authentic dial and decorative tablet arrangements (and fit hinges and a catch to the door). These items can still be obtained from suppliers in the United Kingdom and America.

The original, full-size cases were constructed from comparatively thin material. In this scaled-down version, veneer is applied to both sides of $\frac{1}{8}$ in (3 mm) ply in order to obtain material of suitable finish and thickness. This technique is recommended for all of the case sizes quoted, the ply base being selected to approximate most closely, after veneering, to the required finished thickness.

Choice of Wood

Mahogany was used more than any other wood for the construction of clocks of this kind. Door stiles and rails were cross-band veneered and wood grain on the pediment was sometimes arranged sun-ray fashion – that is, with the grain inclined upwards, at an angle of 45°, on either side of the centre pedestal.

MATERIALS AND COMPONENTS

Cutting List

The following out of $\frac{1}{8}$ in (3 mm) plywood:
- Sides, two off, 4×10 in (102×254 mm)
- Top, one off, $4\frac{1}{4} \times 8$ in (108×203 mm)
- Back, one off, 8 in $\times 10$ in (203×254 mm)
- Case bottom, one off, $6\frac{1}{4} \times 3$ in (160×76 mm)
- Pediment, two off, $3\frac{1}{4} \times 2\frac{1}{2}$ in (83×64 mm)
- Plinth front and back, two off, $8\frac{1}{2} \times 1\frac{1}{2}$ in (216×38 mm)
- Plinth sides, two off, $4\frac{1}{4} \times 1\frac{1}{2}$ in (108×38 mm)
- Plinth top, one off, $4\frac{1}{4} \times 8\frac{1}{4}$ in (108×210 mm)
- Dial board, one off, $6\frac{1}{4} \times 10$ in (160×254 mm)

- Packing between plinth and case: $\frac{1}{4}$ in (6 mm) ply plus two layers of veneer to give $\frac{5}{16}$ in (8 mm) thickness, one off, $4\frac{1}{4} \times 8\frac{1}{4}$ in (108×210 mm)

Strips, in the following *finished* sizes:
- Door stiles and rails, out of $36 \times \frac{5}{8} \times \frac{1}{2}$ in ($920 \times 16 \times 13$ mm)
- Door middle rail, one off, $6 \times \frac{1}{4} \times \frac{7}{16}$ in ($152 \times 6 \times 11$ mm)
- Fillet, to form door top rebate, one off, $6\frac{1}{4} \times \frac{3}{8} \times \frac{3}{8}$ in ($160 \times 9 \times 9$ mm)
- Plinth mouldings, out of $21 \times \frac{9}{32} \times \frac{9}{32}$ in ($530 \times 7 \times 7$ mm)

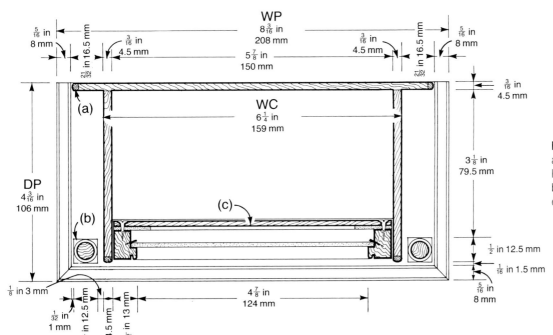

Fig 107 Sectional plan of pillar and scroll clock: (a) rounded lipping to sheet edge; (b) pillar base; (c) door, glass, dial and dial board assembly.

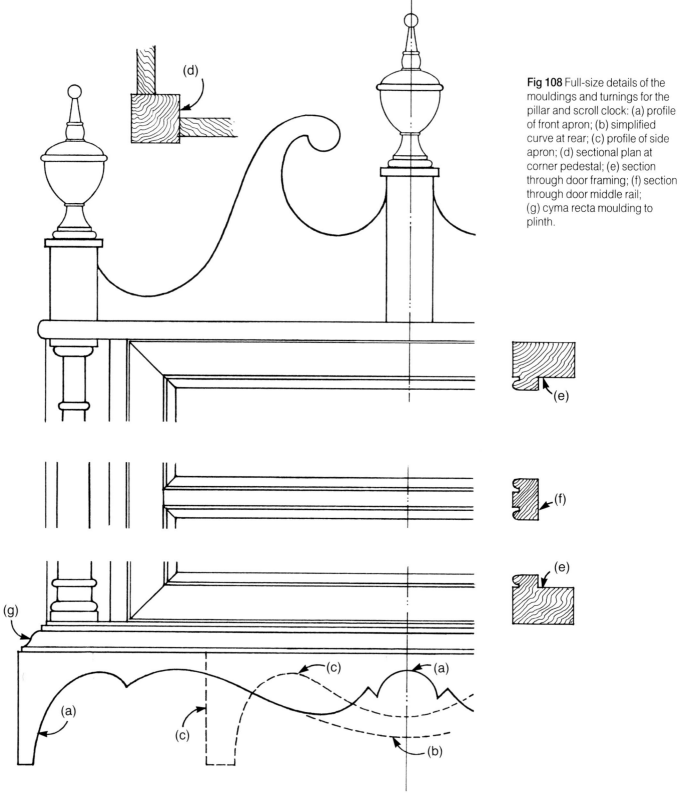

Fig 108 Full-size details of the mouldings and turnings for the pillar and scroll clock: (a) profile of front apron; (b) simplified curve at rear; (c) profile of side apron; (d) sectional plan at corner pedestal; (e) section through door framing; (f) section through door middle rail; (g) cyma recta moulding to plinth.

- Urn pedestals, out of $6 \times \frac{1}{2} \times \frac{1}{2}$ in ($152 \times 13 \times 13$ mm)
- Urns and columns, out of $30 \times \frac{7}{8} \times \frac{7}{8}$ in ($760 \times 22 \times 22$ mm)
- Lippings, out of $60 \times \frac{1}{4} \times \frac{1}{4}$ in ($1,520 \times 6 \times 6$ mm)
- Pedestal caps, column caps and bases, side kerbs to case top, and movement packing piece out of scrap
- Full leaf of veneer 96×9 in ($2,440 \times 230$ mm)

OTHER MATERIALS AND COMPONENTS

- Quartz pendulum movement
- Card dial and hands
- Mounting card and pictorial material
- Brass strip for pendulum rod, $4 \times \frac{3}{16} \times .032$ in ($102 \times 5 \times 0.8$ mm)
- Pendulum bob out of thin (.016 in or 0 4 mm) brass sheet
- Brass strip for movement fixing brackets, $3 \times \frac{3}{4} \times .032$ in ($76 \times 19 \times 0.8$ mm)
- Brass screws:
  Twelve $\frac{3}{8}$ in (9 mm) No. 4 for the dial assembly
  Four $\frac{1}{4}$ in (6 mm) No. 4 for the movement brackets
  One $\frac{3}{4}$ in (19 mm) No. 6 to retain the door
- Two brass escutcheon pins
- Moulding pins, $\frac{1}{2}$ in (13 mm)
- Glass and glazing sprigs

CONSTRUCTION

Veneer both sides of the plywood case parts (this is best done after they have been cut from the sheet), then plane the pieces true, square and to size and glue the lippings in position. Very carefully plane the lippings down flush with the veneer surface. The top is lipped on three sides and mitres are formed at the front corners. Round the lippings slightly.

Only the outer faces of the plinth are veneered, after it has been assembled, in order to hide the butt joints.

Construct the case and the plinth as separate units, then glue the two sections together. The ply parts are held in place while the glue hardens by means of moulding pins driven into pre-bored holes.

Make the square top and bottom pieces for the columns, then turn the columns to fit the vertical gap. Build up the pediment on the case top. Turn four urns, select the two which are the most perfect match, and place them on the outer pedestals. The centre urn should be the same size or very slightly larger, not smaller.

Construct the door frame: note that the glass passes behind the middle rail.

The dial board is fixed to the door frame by means of twelve No. 4 screws, and the dial and mounting card are sandwiched between board and frame. The entire door, dial and movement assembly is held in place by two brass pegs (sawn-off escutcheon pins) at the top and a $\frac{3}{4}$ in (19 mm) screw driven up through the plinth.

A full-size drawing of the mouldings, turnings and decorative parts is given in Fig. 108. Details of the dial and pendulum are given in earlier chapters.

Alternative case dimensions to suit a range of time-ring diameters are given in the table.

	CLOCK DIMENSION		TIME-RING DIAMETERS				
			4 in 102 mm	5 in 127 mm	6 in 152 mm	8 in 203 mm	10 in 254 mm
HC	HEIGHT OF CASE	in mm	$9\frac{3}{4}$ 248	$12\frac{1}{4}$ 311	$14\frac{1}{2}$ 368	$18\frac{1}{2}$ 470	$21\frac{1}{2}$ 546
HP	HEIGHT OF PLINTH	in mm	$1\frac{7}{16}$ 37	2 51	$2\frac{3}{8}$ 60	3 76	$3\frac{1}{2}$ 89
WC	WIDTH OF CASE	in mm	$6\frac{1}{4}$ 159	$7\frac{1}{2}$ 190	$8\frac{7}{8}$ 225	$11\frac{1}{2}$ 292	$13\frac{1}{4}$ 337
WP	WIDTH OF PLINTH	in mm	$8\frac{3}{16}$ 208	$9\frac{3}{4}$ 248	$11\frac{3}{8}$ 289	$14\frac{1}{4}$ 362	$16\frac{1}{2}$ 419
DC	DEPTH OF CASE	in mm	$3\frac{13}{16}$ 97	$3\frac{7}{8}$ 98	4 102	4 102	$4\frac{3}{16}$ 106
DP	DEPTH OF PLINTH	in mm	$4\frac{3}{16}$ 106	$4\frac{1}{4}$ 108	$4\frac{7}{16}$ 113	$4\frac{1}{2}$ 114	$4\frac{3}{4}$ 121
	COLUMN TOP DIAMETER	in mm	$\frac{1}{4}$ 6	$\frac{1}{4}$ 6.5	$\frac{5}{16}$ 7.5	$\frac{3}{8}$ 9.5	$\frac{7}{16}$ 11
	COLUMN BASE DIAMETER	in mm	$\frac{3}{8}$ 9	$\frac{7}{16}$ 11	$\frac{1}{2}$ 13	$\frac{5}{8}$ 16	$\frac{3}{4}$ 19
A	CENTRE PEDESTAL HEIGHT	in mm	$1\frac{1}{2}$ 38	$1\frac{3}{4}$ 45	$2\frac{1}{8}$ 54	$2\frac{5}{8}$ 67	$3\frac{1}{8}$ 79
	PLINTH MOULDING	in mm	$\frac{9}{32} \times \frac{9}{32}$ 7 × 7	$\frac{9}{32} \times \frac{9}{32}$ 7 × 7	$\frac{11}{32} \times \frac{11}{32}$ 9 × 9	$\frac{3}{8} \times \frac{3}{8}$ 9.5 × 9.5	$\frac{7}{16} \times \frac{7}{16}$ 11 × 11
B	DOOR STILES	in mm	$\frac{5}{8} \times \frac{1}{2}$ 16 × 13	$\frac{5}{8} \times \frac{5}{8}$ 16 × 16	$\frac{5}{8} \times \frac{3}{4}$ 16 × 19	$\frac{3}{4} \times 1$ 19 × 25	$\frac{3}{4} \times 1\frac{1}{8}$ 19 × 29
	CASE PANEL THICKNESS	in mm	$\frac{3}{16}$ 4.5	$\frac{3}{16}$ 4.5	$\frac{1}{4}$ 6	$\frac{5}{16}$ 8	$\frac{3}{8}$ 9.5

The Sharp Gothic Clock

HISTORY AND DERIVATION

America experienced a revival of the Gothic style during the nineteenth century. The architect Andrew Jackson Downing carried a torch for Gothic, just as Pugin had done in England, and the Connecticut clockmakers responded to the new fashion with characteristic ingenuity and flair.

They developed two basic designs. First, the round Gothic, with the same profile as the English lancet case. This style came to be known as the beehive clock. Secondly, the sharp Gothic, with a sharp-pointed top flanked by pinnacles. Known as the steeple clock, it was introduced by Elias Ingraham early in the 1840s, and was widely copied by Seth Thomas, Chauncey Jerome and other American clockmakers. A very popular case style, it remained in production until the close of the nineteenth century.

These cases ranged in height between about 19 in (480 mm) and 33 in (840 mm), with around 21 in (530 mm) being common. Case depth was about 4 in (100 mm), measured over the plinth.

GENERAL DETAILS OF THE DESIGN

The clock is shown in the photograph on page 128 and in Figs. 109, 110, 111 and 112. Top pieces inclined at 55° rounded mouldings framing the front of the case, square section bases for the finials and the arrangement of the door panels are details which seldom varied. Manufacturers did, however, adopt a range of finials and base moulding profiles, and typical alternatives are given in Fig. 109. The rather bold, bull-nosed base moulding

included in this design was much favoured by Seth Thomas, a clockmaker of Plymouth Hollow (subsequently renamed Thomaston), Connecticut, who featured it on several of his designs for smaller cases.

The finial bases have been made flush with the sides of the case on this scaled-down replica, but on the full-size originals they often projected $\frac{1}{8}$ in (3 mm) to $\frac{3}{16}$ in (5 mm). The finial base sizes for the two larger clocks, quoted in the table on page 133, allow for a side overhang.

The glazed false door is glued in position and access to

Fig 109 Front view of sharp Gothic clock with alternative finial and base moulding details.

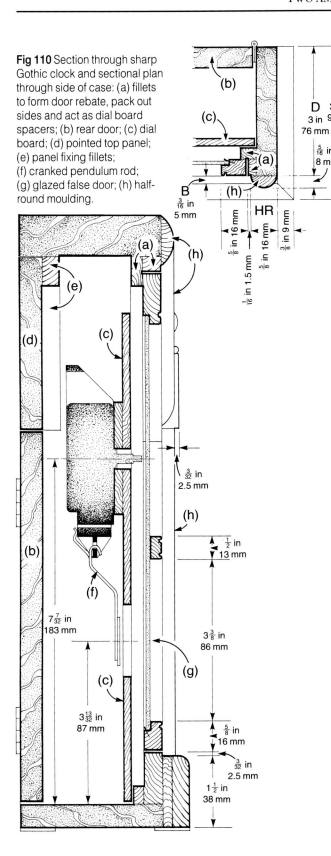

Fig 110 Section through sharp Gothic clock and sectional plan through side of case: (a) fillets to form door rebate, pack out sides and act as dial board spacers; (b) rear door; (c) dial board; (d) pointed top panel; (e) panel fixing fillets; (f) cranked pendulum rod; (g) glazed false door; (h) half-round moulding.

the interior is via a rear door and a removable panel above it. As with the previous design, and for the same reasons, full-size case depth has been more or less maintained on the scaled-down versions.

Choice of Wood

Mahogany veneer was widely used for these clocks but rosewood examples were not unknown. Door stiles and rails, and the rounded mouldings which frame the case, were usually cross-banded – that is, the veneer was laid with the grain running across, not along, the length of the member. The manufacturers used presses to apply veneer in this way to curved profiles and the feature would be difficult to duplicate without special equipment, even using modern impact adhesives. The problem does not arise here because the door members and mouldings are made from solid hardwood, as indeed were these items on some of the full-size originals.

MATERIALS AND COMPONENTS

Cutting List

The case was constructed from plywood and veneered. Constructors wishing to use solid wood should substitute $\frac{1}{2}$ in (13 mm) finished thickness material for the plywood and delete the veneer.

The following out of $\frac{1}{2}$ in (13 mm) thick plywood:
- Sides, two off, $3\frac{1}{4} \times 8\frac{1}{4}$ in (83 × 210 mm)
- Top, two off, $3\frac{1}{4} \times 5\frac{1}{2}$ in (83 × 140 mm)
- Bottom, one off, $3\frac{1}{4} \times 6\frac{1}{4}$ in (83 × 160 mm)
- Rear door, one off, $5\frac{1}{4} \times 8\frac{1}{4}$ in (133 × 210 mm)
- Rear apex, one off, out of $5\frac{1}{4} \times 3\frac{3}{4}$ in (133 × 95 mm)
- Dial board, one off, $\frac{3}{8}$ in (9 mm) plywood, $5\frac{1}{4} \times 12$ in (133 × 305 mm)

Strips, in the following *finished* sizes:
- Base mouldings, out of $18 \times \frac{3}{8} \times 1\frac{1}{2}$ in (460 × 9 × 38 mm)
- Half-round mouldings, out of $30 \times \frac{5}{8} \times \frac{5}{16}$ in (760 × 16 × 8 mm)
- Door stiles and rails, out of $36 \times \frac{3}{8} \times \frac{5}{8}$ in (920 × 9 × 16 mm)
- Door middle rail, one off, $5 \times \frac{1}{4} \times \frac{1}{2}$ in (127 × 6 × 13 mm)
- Finial bases, two off, out of $4 \times \frac{11}{16} \times \frac{11}{16}$ in (102 × 18 × 18 mm)
- Finials, two off, out of $9 \times 1 \times 1$ in (230 × 25 × 25 mm)

- Pack, between door and case sides and top, out of $30 \times \frac{3}{16} \times \frac{3}{8}$ in ($760 \times 5 \times 9$ mm)
- Packing piece behind base moulding, one off, $6\frac{1}{2} \times \frac{3}{16} \times 1\frac{1}{2}$ in ($165 \times 5 \times 38$ mm)
- Base upstand, one off, $5\frac{1}{2} \times \frac{3}{8} \times 1\frac{3}{32}$ in ($140 \times 9 \times 27.5$ mm)

- Dial board spacers, and door stop lath, out of $39 \times \frac{3}{8} \times \frac{1}{4}$ in ($990 \times 9 \times 6$ mm)
- Rear apex fixing fillets, out of $12 \times \frac{3}{8} \times \frac{3}{8}$ in ($305 \times 9 \times 9$ mm)
- Movement packing piece from scrap
- Short leaf of veneer, 36×5 in (920×127 mm)

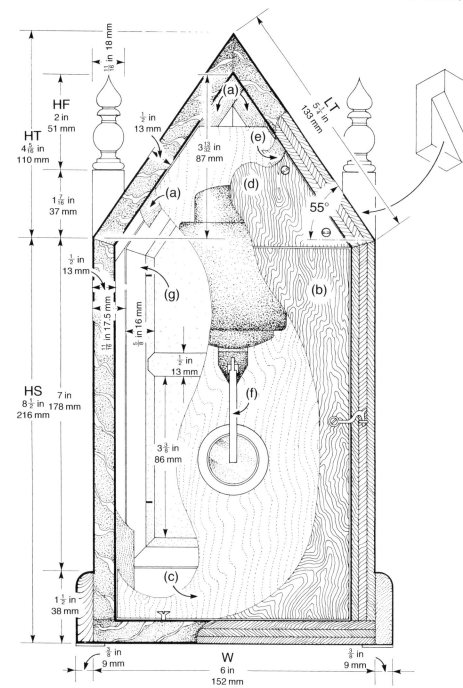

Fig 111 Rear view of sharp Gothic case cut away in layers to expose construction: (a) fillet to form front door rebate and dial board spacer; (b) rear door; (c) dial board; (d) pointed top panel; (e) panel fixing fillets; (f) pendulum rod; (g) glazed false door. Isometric view of finial base shows method of housing this component over the sloping top panel.

Fig 112 Full-size detail of finial to sharp Gothic clock.

OTHER MATERIALS AND COMPONENTS

- Quartz pendulum movement
- Hands and card dial
- Pictorial material for bottom panel
- Brass strip for pendulum rod, $4 \times \frac{3}{16} \times .032$ in ($102 \times 5 \times 0.8$ mm)
- Pendulum bob out of thin (.016 or 0.4 mm) brass sheet
- Brass strip for movement fixing brackets, $3 \times \frac{3}{4} \times .032$ in ($76 \times 19 \times 0.8$ mm)
- Six $\frac{3}{4}$ in (19 mm) No. 6 brass screws for securing the rear panel to the pointed top
- Four $\frac{1}{2}$ in (13 mm) No. 6 brass screws for retaining the dial board
- Four $\frac{1}{4}$ in (6 mm) No. 4 brass screws for securing the movement fixing brackets
- Pair $\frac{3}{4}$ in (19 mm) brass hinges, complete with screws
- Hook-and-eye fastener, $\frac{3}{4}$ in (19 mm)
- Moulding pins
- Glass and glazing sprigs

CONSTRUCTION

The basic box is easier to assemble if the job is tackled in two stages. First, glue and cramp the sides to the base, checking that the assembly is true and square and the sides are parallel. It may be necessary to cramp spacer pieces between the sides to ensure this.

Glue fillets for the apex piece to the top panels, then glue the top panels together. Fix the apex piece to hold the panels in position and at the correct angle. When the adhesive has hardened, glue this assembly to the sides.

Plywood construction makes things easier because moulding pins can be used to hold the parts together while the glue hardens. They must, however, be punched down and the holes carefully stopped; otherwise they will ghost through the veneer.

A splayed halving must be formed at the backs of the finial bases to house them on to the sloping top. Fig. 111 includes a detail of this. Glue the bases in position, then disc-sand the half-round mouldings to length to fit snugly against them.

Two sets of fillets are fixed around the inside front of the cases, one to thicken out the sides, the other to act as dial board spacers and to form a rebate to accommodate the false door.

Alternative case dimensions for a range of time-ring diameters are given in the table.

CLOCK DIMENSION			TIME-RING DIAMETERS		
			3 in / 76 mm	4 in / 102 mm	5 in / 127 mm
HS	HEIGHT OF SIDE	in	$8\frac{1}{2}$	$11\frac{3}{8}$	14
		mm	216	289	356
HT	HEIGHT OF TOP	in	$4\frac{5}{16}$	$5\frac{3}{4}$	$7\frac{1}{8}$
		mm	110	146	181
D	DEPTH	in	3	$3\frac{1}{2}$	4
		mm	76	89	102
W	WIDTH	in	6	8	10
		mm	152	203	254
LT	LENGTH OF TOP PIECE	in	$5\frac{1}{4}$	7	$8\frac{23}{32}$
		mm	133	178	221
HF	HEIGHT OF FINIAL	in	2	$2\frac{3}{4}$	$3\frac{1}{4}$
		mm	51	70	82
	FINIAL PEDESTAL	in	$\frac{11}{16} \times \frac{11}{16} \times 1\frac{7}{16}$	$1\frac{1}{16} \times 1\frac{1}{16} \times 2$	$1\frac{3}{8} \times 1\frac{3}{8} \times 2\frac{1}{2}$
		mm	$18 \times 18 \times 37$	$27 \times 27 \times 51$	$35 \times 35 \times 63$
	BASE MOULDING	in	$\frac{3}{8} \times 1\frac{1}{2}$	$\frac{7}{16} \times 2$	$\frac{1}{2} \times 2\frac{1}{4}$
		mm	9×38	11×51	13×57
	DOOR STILES	in	$\frac{3}{8} \times \frac{5}{8}$	$\frac{3}{8} \times \frac{13}{16}$	$\frac{1}{2} \times 1$
		mm	9×16	9×21	13×25
HR	HALF ROUND MOULDING	in	$\frac{5}{8}$	$\frac{15}{16}$	$1\frac{1}{8}$
		mm	16	24	29
	FRONT DOOR WIDTH	in	$4\frac{5}{8}$	6	$7\frac{1}{2}$
		mm	117	152	190
B	BASE PACKING	in	$\frac{3}{16} \times 1\frac{1}{2}$	$\frac{5}{16} \times 2$	$\frac{3}{8} \times 2\frac{1}{4}$
		mm	5×38	8×51	9×57

CHAPTER SIXTEEN

An Arts and Crafts Clock

HISTORY AND DERIVATION

The Arts and Crafts Movement originated in England during the second half of the nineteenth century. Concerned with the dehumanizing effects of the machine and the importance of craftsmanship, it was a philosophical approach to the decorative arts rather than a style. Nevertheless, things designed in accordance with its principles do have identifiable characteristics, such as simplicity of line and natural materials.

John Ruskin inspired the movement with his writings, but it was William Morris, a firm believer in the concept of the craftsman-designer, who secured its popularity. Architects Arthur Mackmurdo and Charles Voysey were influential followers, and clock cases by Voysey are in the Victoria and Albert Museum and the Geffrye Museum, London.

In America, Elbert Hubbard, the entrepreneur who established the Roycroft workshops, was instrumental in spreading the movement's ideals, but the most important figure was the craftsman-designer Gustav Stickley, whose furniture was popularly known as Mission Oak.

Mantel clocks designed by Voysey and others ranged in height from about 13 in (330 mm) to 22 in (560 mm).

The Arts and Crafts clock. Exposed tenons and the use of oak are typical features

GENERAL DETAILS OF THE DESIGN

The clock is shown in the photograph on page 135 and in Figs. 113, 114, 115 and 116. Tenons are exposed on the sides and the wedge-shaped pieces which impart a slight taper to the case are very much in the manner of Gustav Stickley. The heart-shaped escutcheon, side piercings and hinge strap finials are Voyseyesque, as is the flattened cyma recta top moulding. Gustav Stickley also terminated hinge straps with a heart shape, but he would probably have considered the escutcheon and piercings frivolous.

He would also have simplified the top moulding into a splay, inclined at about 40° to the horizontal.

Notwithstanding its internationally eclectic flavour, the design does exemplify the Arts and Crafts tradition and these notes should enable constructors to produce a modified case more in the manner of Gustav Stickley, should they so wish.

Fig 114 Section through Arts and Crafts clock with quartz movement ghosted out to expose heart motif: (a) dial board; (b) glazed false door; (c) dial board spacer; (d) screwed fillet; (e) rear door; (f) door stop lath; (g) fillet to form rebate for false door; (h) exposed tenon; (i) pendulum bob.

Fig 113 Front view of Arts and Crafts clock.

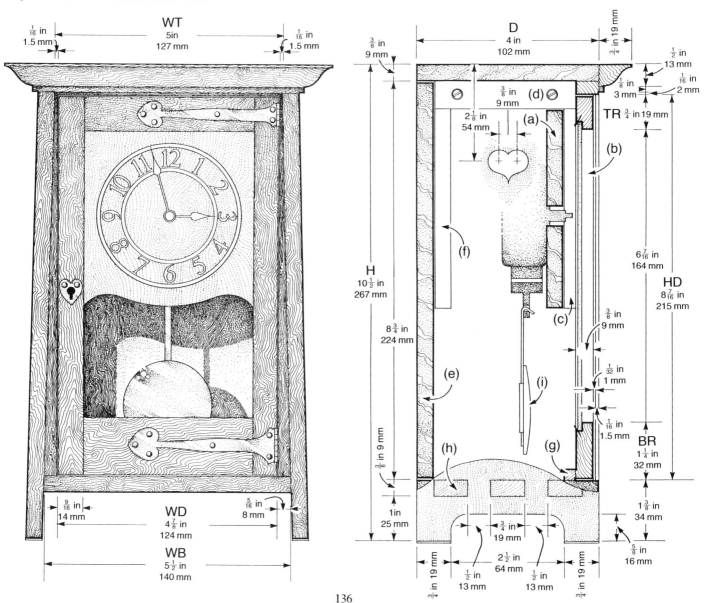

Choice of Wood

Oak, very much the wood of the Arts and Crafts Movement, was used for the construction of the case. Sweet chestnut could be substituted, if desired; after light staining and polishing it would be virtually indistinguishable from oak. Oak veneer could be used, but the exposed tenons would have to be omitted as a feature.

MATERIALS AND COMPONENTS

Cutting List

The following out of $\frac{3}{8}$ in (9 mm) *finished* thickness material:

- Sides, two off, $4\frac{1}{4} \times 10\frac{1}{2}$ in (108×270 mm)
- Top, one off, $4\frac{1}{4} \times 6$ in (108×152 mm)
- Bottom, one off, $4\frac{1}{4} \times 6\frac{1}{2}$ in (108×165 mm)
- Rear door, one off, $5\frac{3}{4} \times 9$ in (146×230 mm)
- Dial board, grain parallel to shortest dimension, one off, $5\frac{3}{4} \times 4\frac{5}{8}$ in (146×117 mm)

Strips, in the following *finished* sizes:

- Top mouldings, out of $24 \times \frac{3}{4} \times \frac{1}{2}$ in ($610 \times 19 \times 13$ mm) and $18 \times \frac{1}{8} \times \frac{1}{8}$ in ($460 \times 3 \times 3$ mm)
- Top packing piece, one off, $6 \times \frac{1}{2} \times \frac{5}{16}$ in ($152 \times 13 \times 8$ mm)
- Top fillets, two off, $3\frac{1}{2} \times \frac{3}{8} \times \frac{5}{8}$ in ($90 \times 9 \times 16$ mm)
- Dial board spacers, false door fillet and rear door stop lath, out of $24 \times \frac{1}{4} \times \frac{3}{8}$ in ($610 \times 6 \times 9$ mm)
- Door stiles, two off, $8\frac{3}{4} \times \frac{3}{8} \times \frac{9}{16}$ in ($222 \times 9 \times 14$ mm)
- Door top rail, one off, $4 \times \frac{3}{8} \times \frac{3}{4}$ in ($102 \times 9 \times 19$ mm)
- Door bottom rail, one off, $4 \times \frac{3}{8} \times 1\frac{1}{4}$ in ($102 \times 9 \times 32$ mm)
- Taper pieces, two off, out of $18 \times \frac{3}{8} \times \frac{5}{16}$ in ($460 \times 9 \times 8$ mm)

OTHER MATERIALS AND COMPONENTS

- Quartz pendulum movement
- Pendulum rod and 2 in (50 mm) diameter pressed brass bob
- Pierced Arabic dial $3\frac{1}{8}$ in (80 mm) diameter
- Brass finish hands
- Brass strip for movement fixing brackets, $3 \times \frac{3}{4} \times .032$ in ($76 \times 19 \times 0.8$ mm)
- Two pairs $\frac{3}{4}$ in (19 mm) brass hinges, complete with screws for one pair
- Brass strip for hinge straps and escutcheon, $9 \times 1 \times .032$ in ($230 \times 25 \times 0.8$ mm)

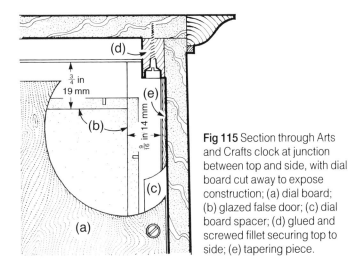

Fig 115 Section through Arts and Crafts clock at junction between top and side, with dial board cut away to expose construction; (a) dial board; (b) glazed false door; (c) dial board spacer; (d) glued and screwed fillet securing top to side; (e) tapering piece.

- Four $\frac{1}{4}$ in (6 mm) No. 4 brass screws for securing movement brackets
- Eight $\frac{5}{8}$ in (16 mm) No. 6 brass screws for securing dial board and case fillets
- Four $\frac{3}{4}$ in (19 mm) No. 6 brass screws for securing case fillets
- Brass hook-and-eye fastener, $\frac{3}{4}$ in (19 mm)
- Brass escutcheon pins
- Glass and glazing sprigs

CONSTRUCTION

Cut out and plane true and square the sides, top and bottom of the case, but leave the bottom piece at its full sawn length at this stage.

With a Stanley knife and set square, mark the lines of the tenon shoulders across each end of the bottom piece, extending them around all four faces. Mark out and saw the tenons, finally cleaning down to the shoulder line with a chisel.

Using the tenons as a template, mark out the positions of the mortises on the case sides. Drill blade entry holes and cut the mortises undersize with a coping saw. Enlarge the mortises to the correct size and clean them up with a $\frac{1}{4}$ in (6 mm) chisel. Test assemble the parts, lightly shaving the mortises and tenons until they are a tight push fit.

Cut the side arches which form the feet and drill overlapping $\frac{1}{2}$ in (13 mm) diameter holes as a preliminary to forming the heart-shaped piercings in the sides.

Glue and screw the fillets to the top piece, then glue and assemble sides, bottom and top. Screws and fillets will hold the sides to the top, but the case should be cramped just above the bottom panel. Check that the diagonals across the tapered front are equal.

Fit the packing piece which is located above the door, cut and fit the taper pieces, then make the door to fit the opening. Remember that the glazing rebates in the stiles will need stopping at the rails.

Plane down the protruding tenons flush with the case sides, then glue the top moulding pieces in position. Make and hang the rear door, which is tapered to fit the case. Glue the remaining fillets and laths in position and cut out and drill the dial board.

The hinge straps and escutcheon are cut from brass strip or sheet. Work close to the profile with a hacksaw and finish with files. The hinge knuckles are a pair of standard $\frac{3}{4}$ in (19 mm) brass hinges, one of which is cut down to $\frac{1}{2}$ in (13 mm) to match the top strap, glued into sinkings in the stile. Drill the escutcheon and straps and hold them in place with dome-headed escutcheon pins, which should be a tight push fit into pre-bored holes. Fit the glass and the

brassware after the final polishing of the case. Apply a spot of black paint beneath the escutcheon to simulate a key hole.

Finishing

Voysey and other followers of the Arts and Crafts Movement used to insist that their oak cases be left bare, without stain or polish. Purists might care to adopt this practice, but the case in this collection was given a light application of medium oak stain and button polished to impart an appearance of age.

Alternative case dimensions for a range of time-ring diameters are given in the table.

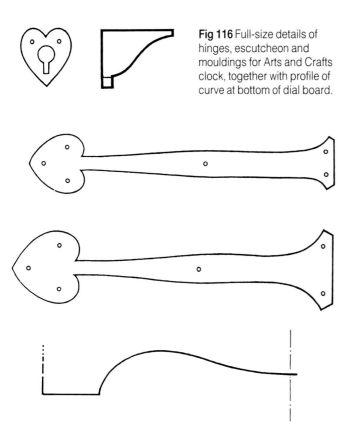

Fig 116 Full-size details of hinges, escutcheon and mouldings for Arts and Crafts clock, together with profile of curve at bottom of dial board.

CLOCK DIMENSION			TIME-RING DIAMETERS		
			3–3$\frac{1}{2}$in 76–90mm	3$\frac{3}{4}$–4$\frac{1}{4}$in 95–108mm	5–6in 127–152mm
H	OVER-ALL HEIGHT	in mm	10$\frac{1}{2}$ 267	13$\frac{5}{8}$ 347	18$\frac{3}{8}$ 467
HD	HEIGHT OF DOOR	in mm	8$\frac{7}{16}$ 215	11 278	14$\frac{3}{4}$ 375
WD	WIDTH OF DOOR	in mm	4$\frac{7}{8}$ 124	6$\frac{5}{16}$ 160	8$\frac{1}{2}$ 217
WT	CASE TOP WIDTH	in mm	5 127	6$\frac{1}{2}$ 165	8$\frac{3}{4}$ 222
WB	CASE BOTTOM WIDTH	in mm	5$\frac{1}{2}$ 140	7$\frac{3}{16}$ 182	9$\frac{5}{8}$ 245
	TOP MOULDING	in mm	$\frac{3}{4} \times \frac{1}{2}$ 19 × 13	1 × $\frac{5}{8}$ 25 × 16	1$\frac{1}{4} \times \frac{7}{8}$ 32 × 22
TR	DOOR TOP RAIL	in mm	$\frac{3}{8} \times \frac{3}{4}$ 9 × 19	$\frac{1}{2} \times 1$ 13 × 25	$\frac{5}{8} \times 1\frac{1}{4}$ 16 × 32
BR	DOOR BOTTOM RAIL	in mm	$\frac{3}{8} \times 1\frac{1}{4}$ 9 × 32	$\frac{1}{2} \times 1\frac{5}{8}$ 13 × 42	$\frac{5}{8} \times 2\frac{1}{4}$ 16 × 58
	DOOR STILES	in mm	$\frac{3}{8} \times \frac{9}{16}$ 9 × 14	$\frac{1}{2} \times \frac{3}{4}$ 13 × 19	$\frac{5}{8} \times 1$ 16 × 25
	CASE MATERIAL	in mm	$\frac{3}{8}$ 9	$\frac{1}{2}$ 13	$\frac{5}{8}$ 16
D	CASE DEPTH	in mm	4 102	5$\frac{1}{4}$ 133	7 178

Notes

1 Case top and bottom widths are measured internally: i.e. *excluding* the thickness of the sides.

2 The top moulding dimension excludes the square-section bead beneath it.

CHAPTER SEVENTEEN

Two Art Nouveau Clocks

At the close of the nineteenth century the decorative arts broke
with tradition and a style developed which became known as
Art Nouveau. Drawing inspiration from natural forms, and with
Celtic and Japanese influences, it was an international
movement with marked regional variations. Clock case design
followed the new fashion, and the two cases described here
reveal how different the approaches to the style could be.

A Clock in the Manner of the Glasgow Four

HISTORY AND DERIVATION

Architect Charles Rennie Mackintosh, his friend Herbert MacNair and their wives, Margaret and Frances Macdonald, made a unique and important contribution to the development of Art Nouveau.

They became known as the Glasgow Four and Mackintosh, the most famous of them, acquired a reputation as a designer of interiors. He and his wife collaborated closely, and their schemes for decorating his often white furniture and rooms involved stylized roses, ethereal female forms and a palette of pink, silver, purple and green.

Margaret and Frances Macdonald produced a large repoussé metal dial, and Mackintosh designed some ungainly black rectangular clocks which seem to have anticipated Art Deco at its least elegant. The inspiration for this case is, therefore, not so much their work on clocks but rather their interiors.

Art Nouveau mantel clocks ranged in size from about 8 in (200 mm) to 20 in (500 mm) high. A clock by Mackintosh, with black stencilled decoration, is in the British Museum, London. Other Mackintosh clocks and associated drawings are in the care of the Hunterian Art Gallery, Glasgow.

GENERAL DETAILS OF THE DESIGN

The case is shown in the photograph on page 139 and in Figs. 117, 118, 119 and 120. The gently rounded top, the curved tapering sides and the bold, sweeping mouldings give the case a sinuous, Art Nouveau silhouette. With its off-white paint finish and stencilled rose decoration, this is very much a boudoir clock.

A brass bezel was fitted but a silver-plated one would have been more appropriate. Constructors who are particularly taken with this design may wish to have a brass bezel plated.

The decorations are reproduced full-size in Fig. 120, and guidance on preparing the stencil and mixing the colours is given in Chapter Four.

Choice of Wood

Any close-grained wood which is stable and capable of being worked to a good finish would be suitable for the painted case. Stock ramin mouldings and pearwood were used for this clock but maple, beech, sycamore or selected knot-free pine would do just as well.

MATERIALS AND COMPONENTS

Cutting List

The following out of $\frac{3}{8}$ in (9 mm) *finished* thickness material:
- Case front and back, two off, $4\frac{3}{4} \times 9\frac{1}{4}$ in (120 × 235 mm)
- Bottom and inner top, two off, $3\frac{1}{2} \times 2\frac{3}{8}$ in (90 × 60 mm)
- Shaped outer top, one off, $5\frac{3}{4} \times 3\frac{3}{4}$ in (146 × 95 mm)

The following out of $\frac{5}{8}$ in (16 mm) *finished* thickness material:
- Sides, two off, $2\frac{3}{8} \times 9\frac{1}{4}$ in (60 × 235 mm)
- Scotia moulding, $36 \times \frac{7}{8} \times \frac{7}{8}$ in (920 × 22 × 22 mm)
- Movement access flap, $\frac{1}{8}$ in (3 mm) plywood, $3\frac{1}{2} \times 3$ in (90 × 76 mm)
- Bun feet, four off, out of $9 \times 1\frac{1}{4} \times 1\frac{1}{4}$ in (230 × 32 × 32 mm)

OTHER MATERIALS AND COMPONENTS

- Quartz movement
- Brass bezel, complete with domed glass and back plate, $3\frac{5}{8}$ in (92 mm) diameter
- Hands and dial-making materials (see Chapter Five)
- Five $\frac{3}{8}$ in (9 mm) No. 6 countersunk brass screws for securing the dial back plate and the access flap

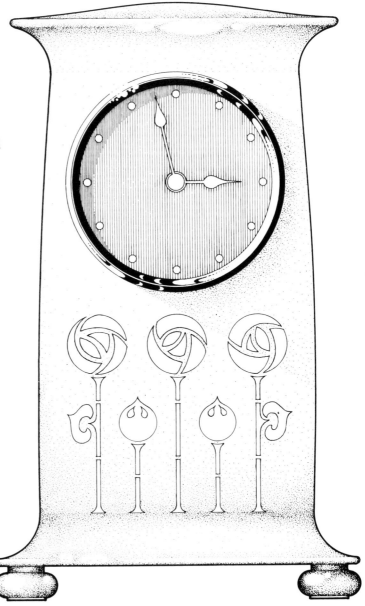

Fig 117 Front view of Glasgow Four-influence Art Nouveau case.

Fig 118 Side view of Glasgow
Four-influence Art Nouveau case.
Case depth is $2\frac{7}{8}$ in (73 mm).

Fig 119 Transverse section
through Glasgow Four-influence
Art Nouveau case.

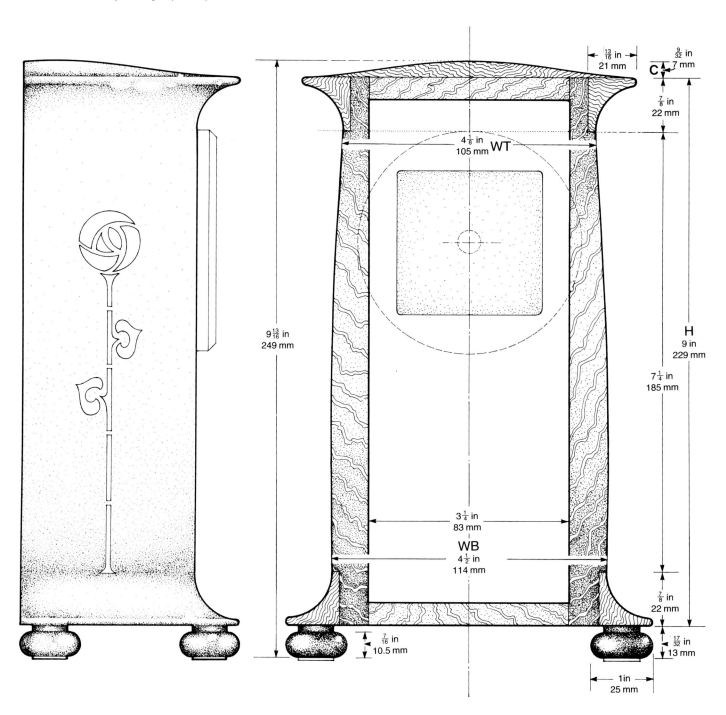

CONSTRUCTION

Build the basic box and then form the tapers on the sides. They should be in continuous, sweeping curves and, ideally, the rate of curvature should increase slightly over the upper two-thirds of the case. Use a plane to remove the bulk of the material and glasspaper down to the final profile.

Form the rebates for the mouldings and glue the mitred pieces of scotia in position. Thoroughly bond the outer top panel to the case; otherwise it will be impossible to work it to smooth feather edges.

As this case is to be painted, modest amounts of filler can be used to mask the joints between the mouldings and the sides, and to hide surface imperfections. Use plastic wood or car-body filler, *not* chalky decorators' fillers. The case must be filled, sealed and sanded until the curves flow smoothly and imperceptibly into one another.

Alternative case dimensions to suit three popular bezel diameters are given in the table.

Fig 120 Full-size details of stencil decorations to Glasgow Four-influence Art Nouveau case.

CLOCK DIMENSION			BEZEL DIAMETERS	
			$3\frac{3}{8}$&$3\frac{5}{8}$in 85 & 92 mm	4in 100 mm
H	HEIGHT CASE	in mm	9 229	$9\frac{3}{4}$ 249
WB	WIDTH AT BASE	in mm	$4\frac{1}{2}$ 114	$4\frac{7}{8}$ 124
WT	WIDTH AT TOP	in mm	$4\frac{1}{8}$ 105	$4\frac{1}{2}$ 114
C	HEIGHT OF CROWN	in mm	$\frac{9}{32}$ 7	$\frac{5}{16}$ 8
D	DEPTH OF CASE	in mm	$2\frac{7}{8}$ 73	$3\frac{1}{8}$ 79
FEET diameter × overall height		in mm	$1 \times \frac{17}{32}$ 25 × 13	$1\frac{1}{16} \times \frac{9}{16}$ 27 × 14
HEIGHT FRONT ROSE		in mm	$3\frac{1}{4}$ 82	$3\frac{1}{2}$ 89
HEIGHT SIDE ROSE		in mm	6 152	$6\frac{1}{2}$ 165

Notes

1 The stencil design can be adjusted to suit a case with a 4 in (100 mm) bezel by lengthening the rose stems slightly and opening out the front decoration so that it lines up with the rim of the larger bezel.

2 Standard $\frac{7}{8}$ in (22 mm) scotia can be used for both sizes of the case, but if larger versions are contemplated, stencil and scotia should be scaled up.

A Celtic-influence Art Nouveau Case

Fig 121 Front view of Celtic-influence Art Nouveau case.

HISTORY AND DERIVATION

The distinctive but restrained style of the Glasgow Four is far removed from the dramatic whiplash lines which characterize the more florid French and Belgian examples of Art Nouveau. Even the intertwined motifs of Celtic and Viking art, expressed so boldly in the work of Englishman Archibald Knox, were interpreted by the Four in a subtle and understated manner. This second clock typifies the more vigorous approach to the style.

GENERAL DETAILS OF THE DESIGN

The clock is shown in the photograph on page 139 and in Figs. 121, 122 and 123. Fig. 26 in Chapter Three gives an 'exploded' view of the filler blocks and plywood front and back panels which form the case.

The Celtic influence on its shape and surface decoration is very evident. Combined with swirling plant forms beneath the dial, it perhaps makes the design accord more closely with the popular conception of Art Nouveau.

At a little more than 8 in (200 mm) high, the size of this clock is authentic as designed, and a table of alternative dimensions has not been included – much larger versions of this case would probably be overwhelming rather than eye-catching.

Choice of Wood

Selected pine can be used for the filler strips and blocks between the plywood sheets. The veneer should be capable of being bent around the tight case curves without splitting and its grain should be inconspicuous – a pronounced figure would clash badly with the stencilled design. Makore was laid on this case and proved satisfactory on all counts. However, the dust from this wood can be an irritant and the species should be avoided by anyone who is sensitive to things of this kind. Brazilian mahogany would be suitable, and so would walnut if evenly coloured pieces are selected.

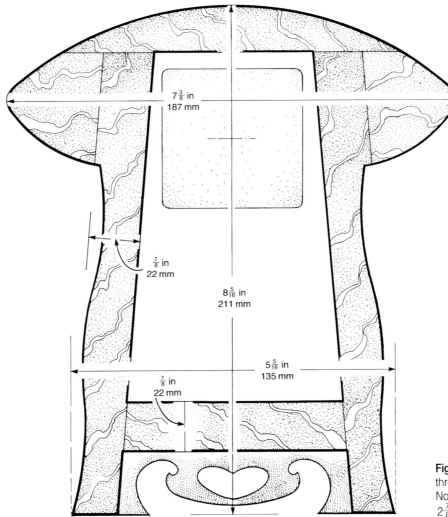

Fig 122 Transverse section through Celtic-influence Art Nouveau case. Case depth is $2\frac{7}{8}$ in (73 mm).

Fig 123 Full-size detail of stencil decoration to Celtic-influence Art Nouveau case.

MATERIALS AND COMPONENTS

Cutting List

- Case front and back, from $\frac{3}{8}$ in (9 mm) plywood, two off, $7\frac{3}{4} \times 8\frac{3}{4}$ in (200 × 222 mm)

Blocking-out pieces in the following, *finished* sizes:
- Sides, top, bottom, out of 30 × $2\frac{1}{8}$ × $\frac{7}{8}$ in (760 × 54 × 22 mm)
- Filler blocks, two off, $2 \times 2\frac{1}{8} \times 1\frac{3}{4}$ in (51 × 54 × 45 mm)
- Movement access flap, $\frac{1}{8}$ in (3 mm) plywood, $3\frac{1}{2} \times 3$ in (90 × 76 mm)
- A short leaf of veneer, 24 × 8 in (610 × 203 mm)

OTHER MATERIALS AND COMPONENTS

- Quartz movement
- Brass bezel, complete with domed glass and backing plate, $3\frac{5}{8}$ in (92 mm) diameter
- Hands and card dial
- Five $\frac{3}{8}$ in (9 mm) No. 6 brass screws for securing dial back plate and access flap

CONSTRUCTION

Detailed guidance on constructing, veneering and decorating this type of case is included in earlier chapters. A full-size drawing of the case profile and decorations is given in Fig. 123. A tracing of the profile can be used to mark out the front and back panels and the design can be traced directly on to the recommended stencil material.

CHAPTER EIGHTEEN

An Admiral's Hat or Napoleon Clock

HISTORY AND DERIVATION

The admiral's hat or Napoleon clock originated in England around 1920 and was manufactured in large numbers over the next two decades by Enfield, Bentina, Smiths and other London firms. The clocks were often equipped with extremely melodious Westminster chimes, and it is likely that the design was developed in order to house extra-long gongs or chime bars without the clock becoming too large, the bars being arranged along the extended floor of the case. It would seem that in searching for a practical solution to a functional problem, the casemakers produced an extremely popular design.

There were many variations to the basic form, ranging from the so-called Jacobean oak to geometric Art Deco cases, and the admiral's-hat-shape was often distorted beyond recognition. Cases in this style ranged in size from about 12 in (300 mm) long and 8 in (200 mm) high to 20 in (500 mm) long and 10 in (250 mm) high, the smaller sizes becoming more popular during the 1930s. The case is undergoing something of a revival in England and America (in America, timepieces of this kind are called tambour clocks), and smaller versions are being added to the original range of sizes.

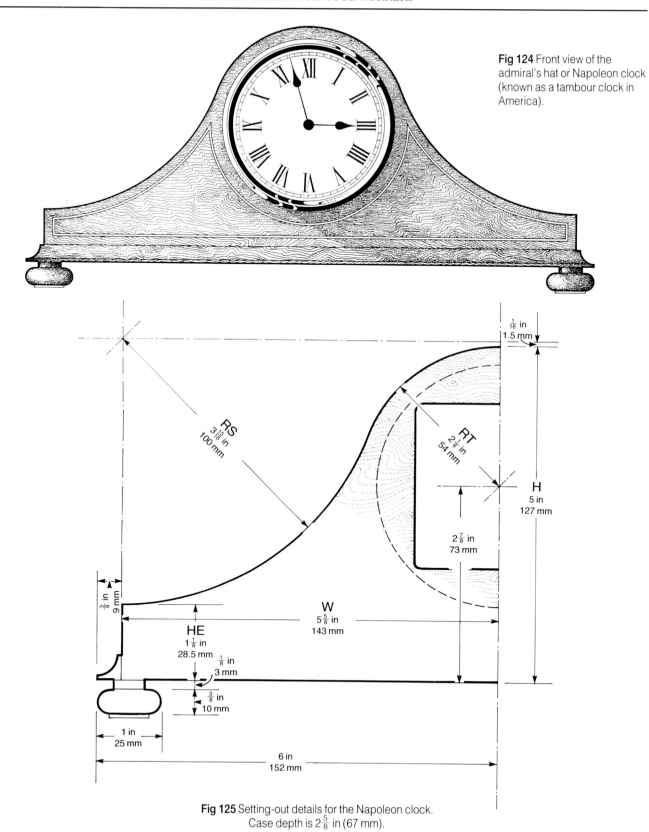

Fig 124 Front view of the admiral's hat or Napoleon clock (known as a tambour clock in America).

RS
$3\frac{15}{16}$ in
100 mm

$\frac{1}{16}$ in
1.5 mm

RT
$2\frac{1}{8}$ in
54 mm

H
5 in
127 mm

$2\frac{7}{8}$ in
73 mm

$\frac{3}{8}$ in
9 mm

W
$5\frac{5}{8}$ in
143 mm

HE
$1\frac{1}{8}$ in
28.5 mm

$\frac{1}{8}$ in
3 mm

$\frac{3}{8}$ in
10 mm

1 in
25 mm

6 in
152 mm

Fig 125 Setting-out details for the Napoleon clock.
Case depth is $2\frac{5}{8}$ in (67 mm).

GENERAL DETAILS OF THE DESIGN

The clock is shown in the photograph on page 147 and in Figs. 124 and 125. It has the sweeping admiral's hat profile and the ends are vertical, in order to form a strong termination to the curving sides. This was a feature of English cases made for Junghans, a German firm based in Hatton Garden, London, during the 1920s and 1930s.

Simulated boxwood stringing and the base moulding echo the sweeping curves of the case, and the turned bun feet are low and of large diameter, to complement its extended width.

Choice of Wood

The original cases were usually veneered in oak, walnut and mahogany, oak being by far the most popular of the three, especially for the less expensive, mass-produced clocks. Mahogany was frequently used for better-quality cases and seems to be the most popular wood for modern reproductions. It was chosen for the case depicted here.

MATERIALS AND COMPONENTS

Cutting List

A built-up block is not really suitable for this case as the horizontal joints would be very obvious on the flattened side curves.

- One-piece block, one off, $12 \times 5\frac{1}{4} \times 2\frac{3}{4}$ in ($305 \times 133 \times 70$ mm)
- Base moulding (scotia), out of $24 \times \frac{3}{8} \times \frac{3}{8}$ in ($610 \times 9 \times 9$ mm)
- Bun feet, four off, out of $9 \times 1\frac{1}{4} \times 1\frac{1}{4}$ in ($230 \times 32 \times 32$ mm)
- Movement access flap, $\frac{1}{8}$ in (3 mm) ply, $3\frac{1}{2} \times 3$ in (90×76 mm)

OTHER MATERIALS AND COMPONENTS

- Quartz movement
- Brass bezel, complete with domed glass and backing plate, $3\frac{5}{8}$ in (92 mm) diameter
- Hands and card dial
- Five $\frac{3}{8}$ in (9 mm) No. 6 brass screws for securing the dial back plate and the access flap

CONSTRUCTION

Construction is described and illustrated in earlier chapters. As with some of the other solid-block cases, the thickness of the block quoted in the cutting list includes a minimal planing allowance, and if a lot of cleaning up is required, the case depth may fall a little short of the recommended $2\frac{5}{8}$ in (67 mm). However, provided it can be kept at or above $2\frac{1}{2}$ in (63 mm), the appearance of the clock will not suffer.

Alternative dimensions for a range of bezel sizes are given in the table.

CLOCK DIMENSION			BEZEL DIAMETERS				
			$3\frac{3}{8}$ & $3\frac{5}{8}$ in 85&92mm	4 in 100mm	$4\frac{3}{8}$ & $4\frac{1}{2}$ in 110&115mm	$5\frac{1}{8}$ & $5\frac{1}{4}$ in 130&135mm	$5\frac{3}{4}$ & 6 in 145&150mm
H	HEIGHT	in	5	$5\frac{7}{16}$	$6\frac{1}{4}$	$7\frac{1}{16}$	$8\frac{1}{8}$
		mm	127	138	159	186	206
W	HALF WIDTH	in	$5\frac{5}{8}$	$6\frac{1}{8}$	7	$8\frac{1}{4}$	$9\frac{3}{16}$
		mm	143	155	178	210	233
HE	HEIGHT OF END	in	$1\frac{1}{8}$	$1\frac{1}{4}$	$1\frac{7}{16}$	$1\frac{5}{8}$	$1\frac{7}{8}$
		mm	28.5	32	36	42	47
RT	RADIUS OF TOP	in	$2\frac{1}{8}$	$2\frac{5}{16}$	$2\frac{5}{8}$	$3\frac{1}{8}$	$3\frac{7}{16}$
		mm	54	59	67	79	87
RS	RADIUS OF SIDE	in	$3\frac{15}{16}$	$4\frac{9}{32}$	$4\frac{15}{16}$	$5\frac{25}{32}$	$6\frac{13}{32}$
		mm	100	109	125	147	163
D	DEPTH	in	$2\frac{5}{8}$	$2\frac{7}{8}$	$3\frac{1}{4}$	$3\frac{7}{8}$	$4\frac{1}{4}$
		mm	67	73	83	98	108
FEET diameter × overall height		in	$1 \times \frac{1}{2}$	$1\frac{1}{16} \times \frac{9}{16}$	$1\frac{1}{4} \times \frac{5}{8}$	$1\frac{7}{16} \times \frac{3}{4}$	$1\frac{5}{8} \times \frac{7}{8}$
		mm	25 × 13	27 × 14	32 × 16	37 × 19	41 × 22

Notes

1 Cases to accommodate $5\frac{1}{8}$ in (130 mm) and larger bezels are best constructed of plywood and veneered.

2 Use $\frac{3}{8}$ in (9 mm) scotia for the base moulding on the two smallest cases, $\frac{1}{2}$ in (13 mm) for the next two sizes and $\frac{5}{8}$ in (16 mm) for the largest.

CHAPTER NINETEEN

An Art Deco Clock

HISTORY AND DERIVATION

Art Deco developed between the two world wars. During the 1920s, stylized garlands, roses, waterfalls and fountains were popular motifs. In the 1930s, the style became abstract and geometric, and sun-rays, zigzags and stepped forms of Aztec origin were common themes. Following the discovery of Tutankhamun's tomb in 1922, ancient Egyptian motifs were revived again and incorporated into Art Deco designs.

Glass, onyx, marble, bronze and Bakelite became the preferred materials for clock cases. In England, the Jaz Clock Company manufactured brightly coloured Bakelite cases in designs considered daring at the time. French designers, whether inspired by naturalistic or abstract forms, produced high-quality clocks, and some of their cubist cases would seem stylish and modern today.

Art Deco mantel clocks tended to be of modest size, normally ranging from some 6 in (150 mm) to 12 in (300 mm) tall.

Fig 126 Full-size detail of the marquetry decoration to the Art Deco clock. The width of the decoration (w), measured at the top of the base moulding, is equal to the bezel diameter. The width of the bands and the difference in height of the peaks (b) is equal to $\frac{w}{14}$.

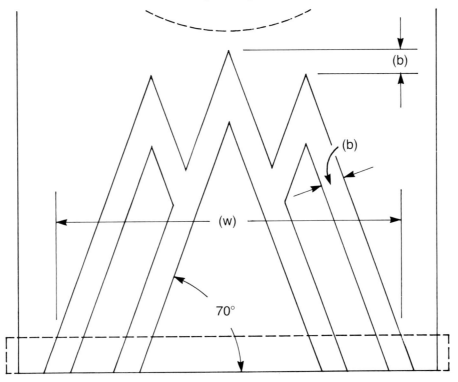

GENERAL DETAILS OF THE DESIGN

The clock is shown in the photograph on page 150 and in Figs. 126, 127 and 128. The stepped top, rectangular base moulding and rounded, projecting feet are conventional Art Deco features. A bold crimson and black zigzag motif is complemented by a black dial with triangular hour markers, the combination being reminiscent of the work of French enamellists of the period.

MATERIALS AND COMPONENTS

Cutting List

The following out of $\frac{3}{8}$ in (9 mm) plywood:
- Front and back, two off, $4\frac{5}{8} \times 7\frac{3}{4}$ in (118 × 197 mm)
- Sides, two off, $2\frac{1}{2} \times 7\frac{3}{4}$ in (64 × 197 mm)
- Top and bottom, two off, $2\frac{1}{2} \times 3\frac{7}{8}$ in (64 × 100 mm)

The following out of $\frac{1}{8}$ in (3 mm) plywood:
- Stepped top, one off, $3\frac{1}{8} \times 4\frac{3}{8}$ in (80 × 111 mm)
- Movement access flap, $3\frac{1}{2} \times 3$ in (90 × 76 mm)

Strips, in the following *finished* sizes:
- Base mouldings, out of $15 \times \frac{1}{8} \times \frac{3}{8}$ in (380 × 3 × 9 mm)
- Feet, four off, out of $6 \times \frac{7}{8} \times \frac{3}{8}$ in (150 × 22 × 9 mm)

Veneer
- Short leaf of harewood veneer, 36 × 6 in (920 × 150 mm)
- Pieces of red and black veneer, each at least 4 × 4 in (102 × 102 mm)

OTHER MATERIALS AND COMPONENTS

- Quartz movement
- Brass bezel, complete with domed glass and backing plate, $3\frac{5}{8}$ in (92 mm) diameter
- Hands and materials for the dial (see Chapter Five)
- Five $\frac{3}{8}$ in (9 mm) No. 6 screws for securing the dial back plate and the access flap

Fig 127 Front view of the Art Deco clock. Case width is $4\frac{3}{8}$ in (111 mm).

Notes

■ Harewood veneer is sold in a variety of shades, ranging from dark grey through to a light silver-grey. A blue-grey variety is also produced (this was chosen for the case). The application of finishes of any kind has a darkening effect, and a lightly stained veneer will help to offset this.

■ Before applying varnish or other finishes to the case, check with scrap pieces of red and back veneer that the solvents will not make the colours bleed.

CONSTRUCTION

Guidance on constructing simple box cases is given in Chapter Three.

Lay the veneer on thin edges first. Veneer the entire top of the basic box, and veneer the piece of plywood which forms the stepped capping before gluing it in position. Veneer the top and front of the length of base moulding before cutting it into individual pieces and forming the mitres.

Alternative case dimensions for a range of popular bezel sizes are given in the table.

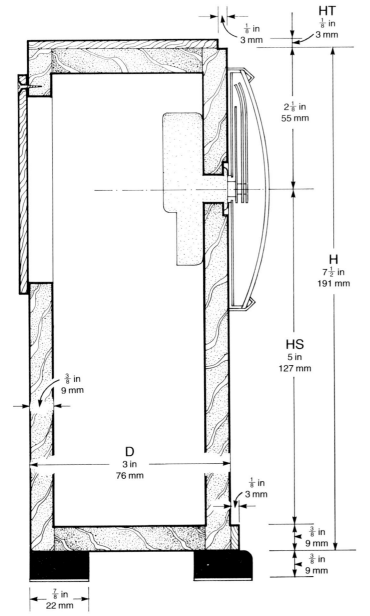

Fig 128 Section through the Art Deco clock.

			BEZEL DIAMETERS		
	CLOCK DIMENSION		$3\frac{3}{8}$ & $3\frac{5}{8}$ in 85 & 92 mm	4 in 100 mm	$4\frac{3}{8}$ & $4\frac{1}{2}$ in 110 & 115 mm
H	HEIGHT	in	$7\frac{1}{2}$	$8\frac{3}{16}$	$9\frac{3}{8}$
		mm	191	208	239
HT	HEIGHT OF TOP	in	$\frac{1}{8}$	$\frac{1}{8}$	$\frac{5}{32}$
		mm	3	3	4
HS	HEIGHT TO SPINDLE	in	5	$5\frac{7}{16}$	$6\frac{1}{4}$
		mm	127	138	159
W	WIDTH	in	$4\frac{3}{8}$	$4\frac{3}{4}$	$5\frac{1}{2}$
		mm	111	121	140
D	DEPTH	in	3	$3\frac{1}{4}$	$3\frac{3}{4}$
		mm	76	83	95
BASE MOULDING		in	$\frac{1}{8} \times \frac{3}{8}$	$\frac{1}{8} \times \frac{3}{8}$	$\frac{5}{32} \times \frac{7}{16}$
		mm	3 × 9	3 × 9	4 × 11
FEET		in	$\frac{7}{8} \times \frac{7}{8} \times \frac{3}{8}$	$1 \times 1 \times \frac{3}{8}$	$1\frac{1}{8} \times 1\frac{1}{8} \times \frac{7}{16}$
		mm	22 × 22 × 9	25 × 25 × 9	28 × 28 × 11

APPENDIX

A Combination Lathe, Disc Sander and Drum Sander

GENERAL DESCRIPTION

The machine comprises a channel-like bed along which can be slid and locked a headstock (powered by the electric drill), a tailstock (the threaded rod and its mounting), a tool rest and a sanding table. Figs. 129–35 detail the lathe arrangement, Figs. 136–9 show the machine set up as a disc sander and Figs. 140–42 as a drum sander.

MATERIALS AND COMPONENTS

The original was built up from scrap material and, provided the basic principles are followed, minor changes can be made to accommodate items which are to hand. Sizes ought not to be indiscriminately reduced, however, as strength and solidity are essential.

A timber and components list is given below. Nominal sizes have been quoted for the various lengths of softwood as this material is usually ordered in this way. The planed or finished sizes, which are about $\frac{1}{4}$ in (6 mm) less, are depicted on the drawings. An allowance has been made in the scheduled lengths and sheet sizes for waste in cutting and finishing.

Pine, spruce or Douglas fir, planed finish (wrot) timber:
- 13 ft (4 metres) of 3×1 in (75×25 mm) for the lathe bed members, feet, sanding table supports and tailstock box
- 6 ft (1.8 metres) of 4×1 in (100×25 mm) for the end brackets, headstock base plate and drum sander stay
- 25 in (635 mm) of 4×2 in (100×50 mm) for the sanding table extended slider

- 18 in (460 mm) of 3×2 in (75×50 mm) for the headstock and tailstock sliders
- Plywood, $\frac{3}{8}$ in (9 mm), 18×30 in (460×760 mm), for the tailstock box, sanding disc and headstock packing
- Plywood, chipboard or blockboard, $\frac{3}{4}$ in (19 mm), $12\frac{1}{2} \times 12\frac{1}{2}$ in (320×320 mm) for the sanding table

The tool rest angle fillet and the sanding table feet can be cut from scrap. It has been assumed that a piece of 4×1 in (100×25 mm) will be thickened out with scrap plywood to form the headstock base plate.

OTHER ITEMS

Countersunk steel woodscrews:
- Thirteen 2 in (50 mm), fourteen $1\frac{1}{2}$ in (38 mm) and sixteen $1\frac{1}{4}$ in (32 mm) No. 12
- Fifteen 1 in (25 mm) and eight $\frac{3}{4}$ in (19 mm) No. 10
- Five 6 in (150 mm) nails
- One 12 in (305 mm) length of $\frac{1}{2}$ in (13 mm) diameter threaded rod, complete with two nuts and two washers
- One $5 \times \frac{3}{8}$ in (125×9 mm) diameter square-necked coach bolt, complete with washer and wing nut
- One $\frac{1}{2} \times \frac{1}{4}$ in (13×6 mm) diameter bolt with $1\frac{1}{2}$ in (38 mm) washer and nut
- One arbor for the sanding disc (fix the largest diameter spindle that can be accepted by the drill chuck)
- One $2 \times \frac{1}{4}$ in (50×6 mm) diameter steel rod and $\frac{1}{8}$ in or $\frac{3}{16}$ in (3 mm or 5 mm) diameter ball bearing (required only if the live or rotating tail stock centre is constructed)
- One radio knob to fit $\frac{1}{4}$ in (6 mm) spindle

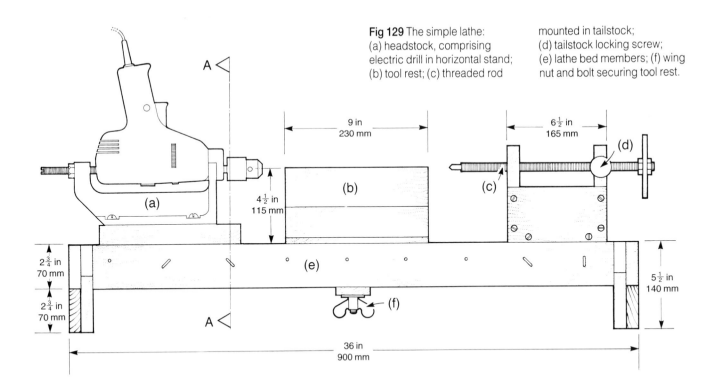

Fig 129 The simple lathe:
(a) headstock, comprising
electric drill in horizontal stand;
(b) tool rest; (c) threaded rod

mounted in tailstock;
(d) tailstock locking screw;
(e) lathe bed members; (f) wing
nut and bolt securing tool rest.

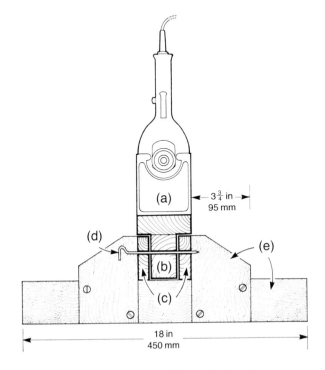

Fig 130 Section through
headstock on A-A: (a) drill in
stand; (b) sliding member;
(c) lathe bed members;
(d) locking pin; (e) end brackets
and feet.

CONSTRUCTION

All of the parts are held together by means of glue and screws. Drill $\frac{1}{4}$ in (6 mm) clearance holes and $\frac{1}{8}$ in (3 mm) thread holes to prevent splitting.

Headstock, tailstock and sanding table are a tight sliding fit between the channel pieces. The sanding table slider is extended to act as a base and bracing member when the machine is arranged in the drum-sanding mode (see Fig. 141). Drill the holes for the drum sander stay pins and fit the stay with the table cramped at 90° to the channel pieces.

The tailstock is a plywood-sided box screwed to a slider block. Fix the electric drill in the headstock and slide the box up to it along the channel in order to drill the holes for the threaded rod. Drill the holes undersize and screw the rod in to cut threads. Remove the head from a 2 in (50 mm) No. 12 screw, attach the radio knob and screw it into a pre-bored hole in a tailstock upright to lock the threaded rod in position. A 4 in (100 mm) diameter plywood disc bolted to the threaded rod acts as a hand wheel.

Point the threaded rod to form a dead centre by holding it at a suitable angle against a grinding wheel or coarse sanding disc running in the electric drill. The rod should be turned steadily to produce an even cone. The more complicated live or rotating centre avoids the need for frequent oiling of the point. Again, mount the electric drill in the headstock and slide the tailstock assembly up to it in order to drill the hole in the end of the rod.

Build up the rigid sanding disc from two sheets of plywood held together by eight $\frac{3}{4}$ in (19 mm) countersunk screws located at 45° centres $\frac{3}{4}$ in (19 mm) from the rim. Remember to insert the arbor and abrasive disc-securing bolt before screwing the parts together. On completion, true up the disc edge in the lathe to remove any slight eccentricity and ensure vibration-free running. The sanding table must, of course, be set at 90° to the disc.

Headstock, tailstock, sanding table and stay are locked in position by means of pins formed from 6 in (150 mm) nails. The nails should be a firm push fit into holes drilled through the channel and sliding pieces.

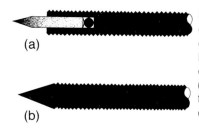

Fig 132 Alternative tailstock centres: (a) live centre comprising a pointed shaft and ball bearing in a socket in the end of the threaded rod; (b) point formed at the end of the threaded rod to act as a dead centre.

Fig 133 Locking pins formed from 6 in (150 mm) round nails.

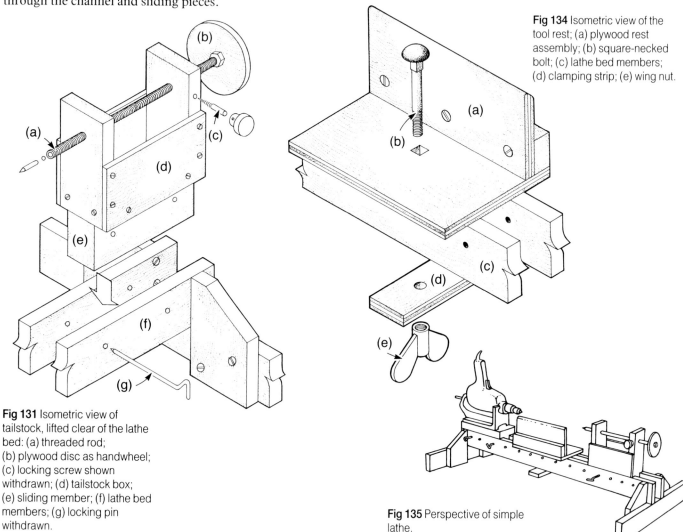

Fig 134 Isometric view of the tool rest; (a) plywood rest assembly; (b) square-necked bolt; (c) lathe bed members; (d) clamping strip; (e) wing nut.

Fig 131 Isometric view of tailstock, lifted clear of the lathe bed: (a) threaded rod; (b) plywood disc as handwheel; (c) locking screw shown withdrawn; (d) tailstock box; (e) sliding member; (f) lathe bed members; (g) locking pin withdrawn.

Fig 135 Perspective of simple lathe.

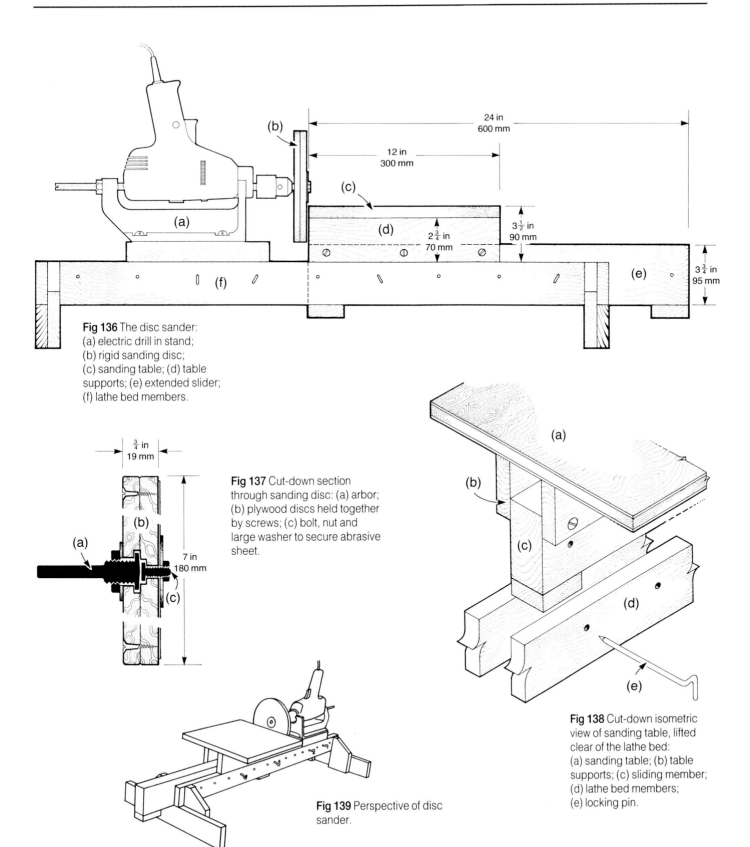

Fig 136 The disc sander:
(a) electric drill in stand;
(b) rigid sanding disc;
(c) sanding table; (d) table
supports; (e) extended slider;
(f) lathe bed members.

Fig 137 Cut-down section
through sanding disc: (a) arbor;
(b) plywood discs held together
by screws; (c) bolt, nut and
large washer to secure abrasive
sheet.

Fig 138 Cut-down isometric
view of sanding table, lifted
clear of the lathe bed:
(a) sanding table; (b) table
supports; (c) sliding member;
(d) lathe bed members;
(e) locking pin.

Fig 139 Perspective of disc
sander.

157

Fig 140 Drum sander locking stay.

Fig 141 The drum sander: (a) lathe bed arranged vertically; (b) electric drill in stand; (c) locking stay; (d) sanding drum; (e) sanding table; (f) extended sliding member; (g) feet to bring sliding member level with lathe bed end.

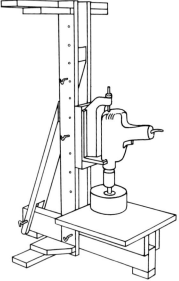

Fig 142 Perspective of drum sander.

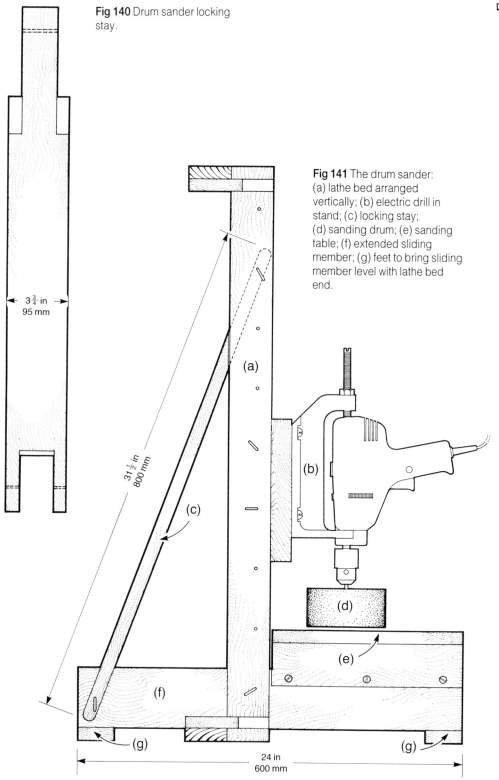

$3\frac{3}{4}$ in
95 mm

$31\frac{1}{2}$ in
800 mm

(a)

(b)

(c)

(d)

(e)

(f)

(g)

(g)

24 in
600 mm

INDEX